Progress and Property Rights
From the Greeks to Magna Carta to the Constitution

By Walker F. Todd

AMERICAN INSTITUTE *for* ECONOMIC RESEARCH

Great Barrington, MA

Progress and Property Rights
From the Greeks to Magna Carta to the Constitution

Economic Bulletin, Vol. XLIX No. 11 November 2009

Published by:
American Institute for Economic Research
Economic Bulletin
250 Division Street
PO Box 1000
Great Barrington, MA 01230
888-528-1216
info@aier.org
www.aier.org

Economic Bulletin (ISSN 0424–2769) (USPS 167–360) is published once a month at Great Barrington, Massachusetts, by American Institute for Economic Research, a scientific and educational organization with no stockholders, chartered under Chapter 180 of the General Laws of Massachusetts. Periodical postage paid at Great Barrington, Massachusetts. Printed in the United States of America. Subscription: $59 per year. POSTMASTER: Send address changes to *Economic Bulletin*, American Institute for Economic Research, Great Barrington, Massachusetts 01230.

Editor: Marcia Stamell

Book Design and Production: Jonathan Sylbert
Cover Design: Jessica Shiner

ISBN 13: 978-091361069-5

Printed in U.S.A.

Preface

All funding for research and preparation of this manuscript was provided by the American Institute for Economic Research. The project was begun under former Director of Research Charles E. Murray and completed after he became president of the Institute. Senior Fellow Kerry Lynch, during her tenure as director of research, reviewed the manuscript and was instrumental in its preparation for publication in the current format. More recently, Creative Director Marcia Stamell reworked the manuscript extensively to enable it to be published in its present form. I am grateful for the support that AIER provided to this project.

—Walker F. Todd, Chagrin Falls, Ohio, November 2009.

Contents

Introduction

Why Do Property Rights Matter?

In the modern world, it increasingly has become clear that the failure to establish and protect property rights goes far toward explaining economic and social underdevelopment. Underdevelopment has proved persistent in countries that retained property rights in a narrow social hierarchy—for example, the typical 1950s Latin American military dictatorship. The same may be said of countries that assigned property rights to no one but the state; that is, to everyone and therefore to no one. The member states of the former Soviet Union are a classic example.

The World Bank, along with associated regional development banks such as the Inter-American Development Bank, the African Development Bank, and the Asian Development Bank, and, to a much lesser degree, the International Monetary Fund, have endeavored for more than 60 years at this writing to promote development (originally in former European colonies) and reconstruction from the ravages of war (principally in Europe and East Asia). The development efforts produced varying degrees of success. Regardless of monetary and budget policies, these efforts generally tended to be successful in the comparatively few countries where adequate legal systems were organized to define and protect property rights and to enforce contracts.

Development has either failed or proved unsustainable in countries where property rights were unprotected or where contracts were unable to be enforced. Gangster states have difficulty in attracting and retaining both investment capital and productive citizens, once the investors and citizens understand that whatever they have can be taken from them by governmental caprice or by bandits operating with governmental approval or acquiescence. There are reasons, in other words, why the north of Italy developed into a modern

European state after World War II. But Sicily and much of the south of Italy remained mired in public corruption and underdevelopment throughout most of the postwar period.

Property rights are essential to achieving the objective of sustainable economic *efficiency*. They promote the material well-being of a larger proportion of the citizenry than would be able to maintain itself above the poverty level in the absence of property rights. Property rights also are essential to the achievement of the moral and political objective of *liberty under the rule of law*. Property supports this because it gives its owners an incentive to create and support political institutions and processes that are conducive to the acquisition, possession, and continued enjoyment of property.

Property can have many definitions. Legal scholar Richard A. Posner, who was appointed to the federal bench in 1981 by President Ronald Reagan, offers this definition in his casebook, *The Economic Analysis of Law*. Referring to Common Law, he divides the rules covering property into three parts:

The law of property, concerned with creating and defining property rights, which are rights to the exclusive use of valuable resources.
The law of contracts, concerned with facilitating the voluntary movement of property rights into the hands of those who value them the most.
The law of torts, concerned with protecting property rights, including the right to bodily integrity.

Posner's definition of property as merely "valuable resources" might seem overly broad. But even the most sketchy analysis soon reveals that the varieties of property to which people give value in economic exchange are so numerous, as are the types of legal protection afforded to their use, that it would be extremely difficult to lay down a hard and fast, universal definition of property. Posner's working definition seems as useful and all-encompassing as any other.

The principal subject of this essay is *general property*, and frequently only real estate or *real property* is meant. The other principal form of legal property that is discussed here is *personal property* or *personalty*, which in law is a broad, general term encompassing, as Posner might put it, anything of value that is not real estate or real property.

Our focus here is on the evolution of the Anglo-American system of property rights. Our review of the period before 1800 is confined to the events necessary to understand the components of the Anglo-American jurisprudential tradition. And because a separate line of evolution of property rights began in America by 1720, the latter part of our review is largely confined to the American tradition alone.

The historical timeline begins with biblical times and extends through the 20th century. It is important to note that early biblical references to property *informed, but did not determine* the distinctive Anglo-American tradition of property rights. It is a frequent mistake to view biblical precedents as the basis for one of the most important features in this tradition, the English (or American) common law. The common law existed among the Angles, Saxons, and Jutes who settled in England even before the country became Christian (after 597). In France, the customs of another Germanic tribe, the Salic or Western Franks, were set down in a legal code that determined property rights more than 70 years before Clovis, their king, became a Christian in 496.

The single most important influence on the evolution of the English common law of property was the set of customs at the time of the Norman invasion (1066) and their modification by William the Conqueror and subsequent English kings. The nobles and later the property-owning non-noble classes struggled to vindicate their property rights by advocating restoration of the pre-Conquest rules. Their political struggles are illustrated by several constitutional documents that include the Coronation Oath of Henry I (1101), Magna Carta (1215), and the Summons of the Model Parliament (1295).

A constant theme of these early documents is that the king may not invade property rights except in accordance with established custom and due process of law. Especially after 1295, both Parliament and the law courts were either interposed between king and subject or granted supremacy over the king in the matters of property rights and taxation.

Principles of taxation are completely intertwined with principles of property rights. As Daniel Webster pointed out to the U.S. Supreme Court in arguing *McCulloch v. Maryland* (1819), "The power to tax involves the power to destroy."

The evolution of English and early American theories of property rights and taxation is traced easily through the Agreement of the People (1649), the English Declaration of Rights (1689), John Locke's *Second Treatise on Civil Government* (1689), the Virginia Bill of Rights (1776), the Declaration of Independence (1776), the Northwest Ordinance (1787), and the U.S. Constitution (1787).

Analogous provisions in French constitutional documents were adopted during the French Revolution of 1789-1795. Through propagation of the Napoleonic Code, these later became the bedrock constitutional documents for most of the civil law countries of continental Europe and French and Spanish North America, including Louisiana, Florida, and the American Southwest.

Much of the philosophical foundation of Anglo-American property rights can be traced back to the views of two great English moral philosophers of the 17th century: Thomas Hobbes (1588-1679) and John Locke (1632-1704). Their views are nearly diametrically opposed.

Hobbes held that the protection of property is the moral basis both of society and of governmental sovereignty over individuals. In his view, the absence of property rights enforced by a strong sovereign would lead to destructive anarchy.

Locke held that individuals acquire property rights through their labor as they apply it to things of nature. In contrast to Hobbes, he argued that property rights precede and are morally superior to the claims of government. Locke also endorsed individual defense of property rights by use of force, while Hobbes preferred that the sovereign have a monopoly on the use of force.

Both Locke and Hobbes agreed that the protection of property rights is the principal objective of society. Locke went further and added that property rights and personal liberty must either march hand in hand or not march at all.

Locke's theory of property rights, rather than the state-centered theory derived from Hobbes, provides support for individual property owners in disputes with political bodies regarding issues such as eminent domain, land-use zoning, uncompensated takings of development rights, and inheritance taxes. Nearly all of America's Founding Fathers were Lockeans in this sense, and the Constitution may be deemed to embody their ideas of property rights.

Unfortunately since the beginning of the Progressive Era in the 1890s, Lockean notions of property rights increasingly have been overridden by courts, legislatures, and executive branch agencies in the name of community interests and the "greater good."

Feeding this assault has been a variety of competing social and economic theories that are part of the Western tradition. The French Revolution introduced new elements into the development of modern notions of property rights. A mere six years after the drafting of the American Constitution, Maximilien Robespierre (1758-1794) laid out a state-centered theory of property rights, rather than one that focused on the rights of individuals, in a famed speech to the National Convention in April 1793.

Robespierre's system also required that a citizen be morally worthy of owning property and enjoying the associated rights and privileges. Inspired by the earlier writings of French philosopher Jean-Jacques Rousseau (1712-1778), Robespierre's ideas became the basis of European socialist doctrines about property.

Other models of political economy have also supported the contemporary erosion of individual property rights. One of these is corporatism or statism (its slightly misleading American name), which is a doctrine that favors a society organized around large, corporate or corporatist bodies such as businesses, trade associations, guilds, and unions, all attempting to control government. Classical corporatism had its roots in ancient Rome, further developed in medieval Europe, and emerged in its modern form in 19th-century Europe. In its extreme or deviant expression, fascism, corporations become the principal organs of state policy and administration. Benito Mussolini in Italy (1883-1945) was the foremost proponent of fascism in the 20th century.

In the United States, a strong variety of corporatism, combined with the beginnings of the modern welfare state, reached its high-water mark in some of the big government programs of the 1930s, especially the National Industrial Recovery Administration (NIRA). Despite the U.S. Supreme Court's 1935 declaration that major components of the NIRA were unconstitutional, the administrative and policy legacies of corporatism have been with us ever since. Some of those legacies found renewed expression in 2008 and 2009 with the various government takeovers and bailouts of financial institutions that accompanied this nation's ongoing mortgage and financial crisis.

Utilitarianism is another view of property rights that runs counter to the classical liberalism of the American founding. Rather than focusing on rights and freedoms for individuals, utilitarianism holds that the aim of society should be to achieve happiness for the greatest number of people or the greatest degree of happiness for the greatest number.

This concept owes its modern philosophical underpinnings to Englishmen Jeremy Bentham (1748-1832), James Mill (1773-1836), and John Stuart Mill (1806-1873). Utilitarianism still has great intellectual appeal to most American-trained economists because of its emphasis on efficiency almost to the exclusion of any other competing value, a condition that they describe as value neutrality.

Since the 1960s, the rise of mathematical expression in academic economics writing has elevated the prominence of utilitarian methodology in public policymaking further because, at its core, utilitarianism relies on calculation of the excess (or deficit) of units of pleasure or pain caused by defined policy choices. Although there are significant experimental aspects of both socialism and corporatism, the mathematical nature of utilitarianism lends itself to experimentation more readily than the other competing political economy models.

As applied to property rights, the main effect of utilitarianism usually is to support the notion that there can or should be "beneficial regulation" of ownership or use of property, which almost inevitably turns into increased levels of state interference in property rights.

The main objectives of this study are both to inform the public of the traditions that underlay the development of modern American property rights and to counteract contemporary trends that seem to be moving away from fundamental notions of individual property rights. The alternative—a state-centered idea of property rights that increasingly dominates the American political landscape—violates traditional constitutional understandings and is directly harmful to individuals and the communities in which they live and work. A knowing and deliberate abandonment of a constitutional understanding might be defensible as public policy, but the defense weakens to the extent that the abandonment is unknowing and unintended.

This study does not claim to reflect the only possible view of the origins and early theories of property rights in biblical and classical times, and it is not intended to be a comprehensive assessment of those origins and theories. Still, the study is a fairly representative survey of the particular lines of development that eventually led to the classical liberal theories of property rights in Western Europe and the United States.

1

Property Rights in the Classical World

The earliest property conveyance in the recorded literature of Western civilization is an oral deed of gift from the Almighty to Adam and Eve and their fellow creatures, as set forth in Genesis 1:28-30:

> Then God blessed them and said to them, "Be fruitful and multiply; fill the earth and subdue it. Have dominion over the fish of the sea, the birds of the air, the cattle and all the animals that crawl on the earth." God also said, "See, I give you every seed-bearing plant on the earth and every tree which has seed-bearing fruit to be your food. To every wild animal of the earth, to every bird of the air, and to every creature that crawls and has the breath of life, I give the green plants for food." And so it was.

The first modern-sounding property transfer recorded in the Bible comes somewhat later in Genesis in Chapter 23, concerning Abraham's purchase of a burial site. Abraham is confronted with the problem of finding a suitable burial place for his wife Sarah, who died at the age of 127. Although Abraham was a sojourner in a foreign land (he was born in Chaldea, at Ur, in modern Iraq) and led a somewhat nomadic existence (he kept herds of sheep, cattle, and camels), his flocks grazed on roughly the same lands. It made sense for him to find a burial place for Sarah close to his normal grazing territory, and a cave at Machpelah (now Hebron) became that site.

Abraham asks the local Hittite nobles for a burial place. It soon becomes clear to him that he must purchase the tomb instead of accepting it as a gift in order to gain unquestioned title. A later king or nobleman might revoke a mere gift. But if Abraham could purchase a plot for full and fair value, completing the transaction in the presence of enough witnesses, then no one would be allowed to question his lawful title to the property afterward.

Ephron, the king, proclaims the value of the land to be 400 silver shekels (about 210 troy ounces of silver), an enormous sum for that day. Abraham accepts Ephron's price and in the presence of all the nobles pays the 400 shekels to Ephron. Genesis 23:16-17 says, "Thus Ephron's field in Machpelah . . . that is, the field, the cave, and all the trees in the entire field, became the property of Abraham in the presence of all the Hittites, his fellow citizens."

The modern lesson from this biblical story is that the common law of real property transfers, and of property rights, is remarkably ancient. The story of Abraham is at least 3,500 years old. Yet Abraham's transaction with Ephron and the Hittites largely resembles the common law of real property transfers at various times and places, even within the United States, before the widespread practice of recording real estate transactions began in the 1800s.

Key elements of a common-law transfer of real property are already present in the biblical account. They include:

Voluntary exchange (Abraham the willing buyer bargains with Ephron the willing, or at least a well-compensated, seller).

An agreed price (proportional requital).

A declaration of transfer in the presence of witnesses (the Hittite nobles), and actual possession and use by the buyer (Abraham buried Sarah in the tomb).

For comparison, in frontier America, young boys might be brought forward to witness a property transfer, as were the Hittite nobles. The legal phrase *time immemorial*, or time outside the memory of those now living, is related to such customs. Years or even decades later, if a boundary or ownership dispute arose, those young male witnesses, now old men, would be summoned to testify about the transfers they saw. Or if they themselves did not witness a transaction, they would be asked who, when they were young, the oldest men *then* living in the neighborhood had said were generally reputed to own the property in question.

Just as Genesis is the earliest tale of property rights in the Bible, Homer's *Iliad* (ca. 800-900 B.C.) provides the earliest such tale in the Greek tradition.

In the story, the Greeks have besieged Troy (Ilium), itself a city of the Greek civilization, for nine years. Troy was a mighty city that had not been sacked in the 300 years of its existence. The attacking Greeks are about to abandon the battle and return home, disgusted with the arbitrary and capricious conduct of Agamemnon, their leader and the chief of the Greek kings, when an interesting scene unfolds.

Helen, wife of the Spartan King Menelaus, brother of King Agamemnon of Mycenae, had been taken by Paris to live in the house of his father, Priam, King of Troy. Achilles and other Greek warriors follow the Greek kings to Troy to maintain the siege and demand the return of Helen. In reality, as Achilles admits, they are there principally for the booty that would come from capturing and then sacking the city. Especially prized are the female captives. Agamemnon, for example, has taken the daughter of the priest of Apollo and will not return her.

The Greeks are then afflicted with plague sent by Apollo in response to the prayers of the priest. Agamemnon reluctantly agrees to release the girl to appease Apollo and relieve the plague, but only if in turn he may have his pick of the female prizes held by the other Greek chieftains. He selects a girl held by Achilles. The Greeks protest that it is unfair to re-divide the prizes once they are awarded.

This protest suggests that a certain respect for property rights among pirates was expected. The passage also illustrates that in ancient Greek civilization the status of women—other than a man's legitimate wife—was at about the level of chattel property. At the very least, when women were taken as prizes in wars, they were treated as transferably as the other most prized loot—gold and silver vessels.

PERSONS AND LIBERTY

Aristotle's *The Athenian Constitution* (ca. 350 B.C.) presents another early account of property rights in the story of Solon of Athens. Solon was archon, Athens' chief official, in the period 594-593 B.C.

In the generation preceding the tale, because of an increase of population, demands on local sources of grain often exceeded the local supply. During this time, most of the people became indebted to landlords, borrowing grain to survive from one season to the next. The loans were made on the security of the person; that is, in case of default, the creditor had the right to sell the debtor into slavery. Entire families who formerly were free became serfs in this manner.

Solon introduced major reforms of debt and property, canceling debts and making it illegal for men to trade their personal liberty for money. His interventions in the Athenian economy were undertaken in the interest of justice and fair play, following what later would be defined as the Aristotelian principle of justice.

Aristotle outlined the three critical components of a just and fair society that Solon first articulated. Forbidding people to borrow money on the security of their own persons was the first of these. The second was the right to legal redress for those who were suffering wrong. The third was the right to appeal to the people's court. Scholars say this final right gave the mass of the people their greatest leverage. It became the core of Athenian democracy because control of the legal process paved the way to control of the constitution.

The Athenian approach to property rights, as described by Aristotle, was by no means universal in ancient Greece. Socrates (469 to 399 B.C.) held that the vision of the ideal state was one without private property, at least among the leaders whom Socrates classified as "philosopher-kings" and "warrior athletes and guardians." The views of Socrates on this matter, which were derived from his acquaintance with the civic organization of Sparta, are summarized in the beginning of Book VIII of Plato's *The Republic* (probably written sometime between 380 and 360 B.C.

The writings of the ancient Greeks were familiar to the more learned of the generation of the Founding Fathers of the United States, particularly men such as Thomas Jefferson, John Adams, and James Madison. Ancient Greek views on property rights influenced the views of those who wrote the first new American laws on property.

One example is the democratic dispersion of property rights. This notion, which is intrinsic in the argument of Thersites in the *Iliad* and evident in Athenian practice after the statutes of Solon, persisted among the common people (the *demos*).

Democratic dispersion of property rights arises in societies that intend to preserve systems of checks and balances against concentrations of money (or other property) and power in order to insure the ongoing viability of democratic institutions. A good illustration of this principle in American jurisprudence is the Rule Against Perpetuities, requiring the distribution to natural persons, as eventual holders, of estate and trust assets within a defined period, usually the life of the youngest beneficiary plus up to 21 years. Jefferson explained the Rule, in an earlier and more idealistic form, in a letter to Washington, as a necessary check against the rise of a titled aristocracy created by the states in the young republic.

The idea of a democratic dispersion of property ownership appears much later and quite strongly in the Northwest Ordinance (1787). This document played a key role in the westward expansion of the United States (and is discussed further in Chapter 5).

THE INFLUENCE OF THE ROMAN REPUBLIC ON THE EVOLUTION OF PROPERTY RIGHTS

The Founding Fathers idealized the austerity and integrity of the old Roman Republic. Historians traditionally date the beginning of the decline of this Republic to the Punic Wars with Carthage, which were waged for mastery of the Mediterranean world. In particular, the end of the Second Punic War (218-201 B.C.) marked a turning point. The Romans survived Hannibal's invasion of Italy by way of Spain and ultimately defeated Carthage. This victory encouraged Rome to pursue an expansionist and imperialistic policy.

The Republic officially became the Roman Empire following the death of Julius Caesar in 44 B.C. The Empire itself fell to the invading Visigoths more than 500 years later, in 476 A.D.

Property relations during the old Republic varied. Outside the immediate territory around Rome, they generally were those of master and slave, with the patricians as masters and the plebeians as slaves. In and near Rome, plebeians had stronger rights. In the early years of the old Republic, which covered a much smaller territory than in the late Republic or the imperial period, the landowners were reputed to be small freeholding farmers. By the end of the old Republic, however, these farmers largely had vanished and became absorbed into the mass of serfs.

The categories of later Roman law of property are constructed, according to the 19th-century legal historian Sir Henry S. Maine, on several layers of principles or theorems derived from Roman conceptions of natural law. The first principle of Roman property law is occupancy, which Maine defined as "...taking possession of that which at the moment is the property of no man, with the view ... of acquiring the property in it for yourself."

The Roman conception of occupancy was a theoretical advance in the law of property rights because, for the first time in the civilized world of the West, enforceable general rules were laid down regarding both unclaimed property and disputed property claims.

Objects that Roman lawyers called "property of no one" apparently constituted specific exceptions to the general principle that all property has an owner. Things that never had an owner included wild animals, fish and fowl, jewels mined for the first time, and lands that were either uncultivated or newly discovered. Also on this list were abandoned lands and objects and, above all, *the property of enemies*.

Despite the apparent harshness, wrote Maine, the unexpected inclusion of "the property of an enemy" as one of the things that belong to no one under Roman law was a civilizing measure. It induced greater respect for the property rights of friendly persons or forces, *once claimed*, instead of the "indiscriminate plunder" that might have occurred in, say, the pre-Homeric age of Greek piracy.

According to 18th-century scholars, the Roman law Principle of Occupancy itself is broken down into three elements derived from occupancy. Occupancy requires that all property rights be "founded on adverse possession ripened by prescription." In other words, occupancy is determined by possession, exclusivity of use (adverseness of possession), and uninterrupted use over time (prescription).

These elements derived from Roman law have become the governing principles of modern property law throughout Western civilization.

2

The Rise of Europe

When the Roman Empire fell in the West in 476, it left behind a system of land tenures that ultimately became the basis for modern property rights in Western Europe. During the later phases of the Empire, first municipalities and subsequently proprietors of private estates began the practice of leasing lands to free tenants who paid shares of their crops over long terms and at fixed rates.

These tenants, whose holdings were regulated by contract with the owners, gradually became recognized by municipal authorities as having a qualified proprietorship, called *emphyteusis*. *Emphyteusis* was a precursor to the feudal system of land tenure. It was essentially a long-term or even perpetual rental that could be transferred and inherited, free of the landlord's right to evict the tenant, upon proof of the tenant's actual use and improvement and timely payment of rent. The landlord's traditional right to take the land back was derived from his ultimate ownership of the residual title. Thus, throughout the Middle Ages, land acquired and retained a form of double ownership.

Along the Rhine and Danube frontiers of the late Empire, veteran soldiers occupied state-owned lands roughly under the terms of *emphyteusis*, with one significant addition: an obligation of military service upon demand of the state, the ultimate landlord. Creating a precedent for feudal land grants, which early on (but not later) carried with them a requirement of such service, the Roman soldier/farmers cultivated their lands with the understanding that they could be called to military service to protect the border. These terms stood in stark contrast to *allodial* proprietorships, in which individuals held land free of any duty of servitude or rental payment to any lord.

After the fall of Rome, the Franks became the dominant force in Europe, occupying central and western Germany, northern Italy, and eastern France. Clovis (465-511 A.D.) became the first Christian king of the Franks in 496 and later gained most of southern France for them. He is credited with commissioning the first written law among the barbarian tribes, the Salic Law or the Salic Code. This law was created for the western Franks, a Germanic people then living in eastern France.

Largely concerned with procedural and criminal matters, the Salic Law also weighed in on inheritances. The most important feature was a passage prohibiting the inheritance of land by women or through the female line. This would significantly impact inheritance rights and royal succession in England after 1066 and in France throughout the monarchy.

In contrast, the inheritance of land by or through women was allowed in England under the Anglo-Saxon common law. The latter custom was superseded, however, when the invasion of England in 1066 brought the Norman French customs inherited from the Salic Code into England. Because of the Salic Law, it wasn't until 1553, when Mary I, half sister to Elizabeth I, ascended the throne of England that a Western European woman ruled in her own right.

Charlemagne (742-814) became the first king of all the Franks after 771 and was crowned Holy Roman Emperor in 800 by Pope Leo III. In the latter years of his reign, the first Norman invasions by the Vikings reached northern France, and Charlemagne began to enforce military obligations as the condition of holding land for all his fighting men. He also required the payment of benefices or grants from his noblemen to the emperor for other lands and concessions. This is the precursor of the medieval forms of taxation of the nobility that are described in Magna Carta (1215).

DEÜST BASTARS TERE HERITIER?
HAS A BASTARD THE RIGHT TO INHERIT LAND?

The Old French epic poem *Raoul de Cambrai* (ca. 1100) is a historically realistic (even if not entirely factually accurate) *chanson de geste*, unlike the vast majority of the "action songs" of the day. In *Raoul*, a rapacious Count of Cambrai is accompanied by his squire Bernier, the illegitimate son of a northern French nobleman. At one point, Bernier aspires to inheriting land in his own right. This prompts King Louis IV (936-954), who was the Count's uncle, to exclaim, *"Deüst bastars tere heritier?"* "Has a bastard then the right to claim a land?"

Louis' question raises the issue of the official position of the Church on the right of illegitimate children to inherit property during the Middle Ages. In *Raoul*, the question is delicately ironic, for the legitimate Count Raoul pillages a convent and orders the nuns raped by the knights' squires, while the illegitimate Bernier embodies all the honorable and chivalric virtues. Nevertheless, under the feudal law of the day, Raoul may inherit land, while Bernier cannot.

In Roman law, a bastard had the official status of *filius nullius*, son of no one, or *filius populi*, son of the people. Bastards were not allowed to inherit land. However, Roman law in the latter phases of the Empire was rather loose with adoption standards, and if a father was willing to marry the mother, or to adopt the child formally, then the child could be legitimized. Without such paternal action, an illegitimate child was stuck with his or her original status, unless a proclamation by the king or an act of parliament declared the child legitimate.

Under most modern American law, illegitimate children are always allowed to inherit from their mothers and from their fathers if paternity is acknowledged or proven in a legal proceeding. Common law marriage used to be recognized in most states as a saving process for avoiding illegitimacy. As statutes have removed the legal disabilities of illegitimate children in recent years, the economic rationale for recognition of common law marriage also has disappeared. In Ohio, for example, no common law marriage inside or outside Ohio since October 1990 may be recognized by law. But there no longer are obstacles to inheritance for children born out of wedlock from fathers whose paternity is recognized by law.

In the Middle Ages, one option for powerful and well-connected bastards was to conquer new estates of their own, using the old Roman rationale that enemy property is the property of no one. That is exactly what William, Duke of Normandy (1027-1087), also known as William the Bastard, did. He conquered England in 1066 and made himself king. He had become the Duke of Normandy in 1035 despite his illegitimate birth (his mother was a tanner's daughter) because the Norman nobles agreed to recognize him as his father's son and lawful male heir.

AFTERMATH OF THE NORMAN CONQUEST: WHOSE LAW GOVERNED?

Traditional English common law has ancient roots in the practices of the Germanic tribes (Angles, Saxons, and Jutes) who settled in England after the

Roman army left in 410. With the arrival of William and the Normans in 1066, the common law tradition often was set aside for Norman French customs.

For several hundred years afterward, the English court maintained records and legal proceedings in Norman French (later, Court French or Law French, a language by then written or spoken nowhere else) as well as Latin, neither of which was the language of the common people of England. Special writs and other practices of Norman French law were introduced soon after the invasion. And the kings began to assert prerogatives against the people and their property that were unknown in common law.

Henry I (1068-1135), youngest son of William the Conqueror, made a successful bid for the throne in 1100 when his elder brother, King William II, died, and his surviving older brother Robert, Duke of Normandy, was away on a crusade. Henry appealed for support to the English nobles, promising them to abolish most of the annoying Norman French laws and practices (which Robert certainly would not have done) in exchange for the crown.

Henry's promises are set forth in the oldest constitutional document of Anglo-American jurisprudence with modern significance, the Coronation Oath of 1100. It was modeled on the coronation oath of King Ethelred II (968-1016), the last English king before foreigners (first Danes and then Norman Frenchmen) began to claim the crown. English nobles were ready to listen to Henry's promises of reform and restoration of ancient laws. His Coronation Oath was confirmed a year later in the detailed Charter issued at his formal coronation ceremony.

The Coronation Charter (1101) promised that the church would be free of the crown for deciding the succession of bishops and that all the "evil customs" of the realm would be ended. Forfeitures of estates to the crown that had occurred under William the Conqueror and William II (king, 1087-1100) were restored to the original owners. Afterward the crown agreed to observe practices regarding forfeitures (usually a consequence of conviction for felonies) that predated the reign of William the Conqueror. Murders prior to Henry's coronation were pardoned, and future murders were to be penalized under the common law, as they were under Edward the Confessor (king, 1042-1066), who ruled at the time of the Norman invasion. By these changes, Henry abandoned Norman legal practices that usually caused estates to be seized from the families of their original owners and forfeited to the crown.

An important stage in the evolution of the Anglo-American conception of property rights was the treatment of forest lands by Henry I. Before 1066, forest lands generally had been common lands. With the coronation of Henry I, forest lands and the game animals within them were kept in the king's own control.

Henry's charter promised knights free tenements (tax free tenancies) so as to enable them to better equip themselves and their men for military service. As a culminating gesture, Henry also restored traditional common law, except as it had been amended by *both* the king *and his council of barons* since that time. Henry decided to honor the memory of his father, William the Conquerer, at least to the extent of keeping legal changes that had been approved by the king's council, which he apparently thought would be more acceptable to the nobles generally, while setting aside changes that the king alone approved.

Many of the same issues treated in the Charter of 1101, including promises to restore the laws of either the time of King Henry I or King Edward, were raised and reiterated 114 years later in Magna Carta. In general, the Coronation Oath and Charter of Henry I state the legal conditions for the occupancy, retention, and inheritance of private property in England, insuring that the common law would govern most such issues. However, alienation (transferability) of land does not seem to have been contemplated, either in Henry's texts or in Magna Carta.

RIGHTS DERIVED FROM CUSTOM: THE MAGNA CARTA

Many of the same issues that provoked the Coronation Oath and Charter of Henry I reappeared over the next century.

Many of the recurring issues in Magna Carta had to do with taxation. English barons chafed at the royal imposition of taxation without their consent. They also objected to the imposition of taxes for customary purposes. They objected especially to the levying of taxes for crusades and foreign wars that never were undertaken. Feudal inheritance taxes were also an irritant. The arbitrary and excessive reliefs, which were equivalent to inheritance taxes that William I and William II had imposed, returned despite the promises of the Coronation Oath and Charter. Many of the most objectionable new practices and laws were derived from Norman French rather than Anglo-Saxon legal customs.

All these issues came to a head June 15, 1215, at Runnymede, a meadow west of Windsor on the Thames River. The English barons met King John with a superior military force and forced the king to sign one of the most important legal documents in the history of democracy, the Magna Carta. With it, John recognized ancient English liberties and placed himself and his heirs under the rule of law. Despite occasional backsliding, the English monarchy generally has continued to recognize the same set of ancient liberties of the subject as well as the supremacy of law over the royal sovereign himself.

King John later tried to disavow his signature on Magna Carta, writing to the Pope to ask for dispensation from having to observe the oaths that he delivered under compulsion or duress. The Pope granted the dispensation. However, John died the next year before the papal letter of absolution arrived from Rome. John's son, Henry III, became king and reissued Magna Carta in 1217.

Magna Carta spells out liberties brought to the New World four centuries later by the English colonists. Their descendants ultimately fought for these rights and liberties in the American Revolution and restated them in both the Declaration of Independence and the U.S. Constitution.

Magna Carta is not explicitly part of the Constitution. However, the original constitutions and early judiciary acts of the states usually provided that the common law of England was the common law of any particular state until that law was changed positively, as by statutory enactment.

Building on the foundation of the Coronation Oath and Charter of Henry I, the document shows what that common law was intended to be. Magna Carta contains 63 paragraphs. Among the freedoms it delineates are the right to due process of law, freedom from unlawful imprisonment, and the freedom of the English Church to function without interference from the government. But the primary concerns of this Great Charter of English freedom are property rights, inheritances, and taxation.

Notable provisions of Magna Carta include the re-establishment of the ancient fee schedule for reliefs, which gave the nobles increased confidence that their heirs could inherit their estates. In classical economic theory, this confidence in the capacity to build estates that can be passed to descendants contributes to active management of estates for improvement instead of to a desire to consume the estate during a lifetime. Another area that Magna Carta covers, overturning the Norman French tradition, is recognition of the customary rights of widows to their inheritances from their own families and from their dower on the deaths of their husbands, including a 40-day respite in paying rent.

The charter also limits royal taxation to three customary cases—ransoming the king's person, the knighting of the king's eldest son, and the first marriage of the king's eldest daughter—and prohibits any nobleman from assessing his own tenants for any but the same three occasions in the nobleman's life.

Magna Carta is a guarantee of the property rights of free inhabitants of the British Isles and their descendants, forever, with respect to the British crown. It envisions private property rights (as opposed to communal rights) as existing without substantial state interference with their enjoyment. It establishes that property cannot be taken by the sovereign without the consent of the owner (a weak principle that later had to be strengthened regarding just compensation) or without due process of law. Finally, Magna Carta asserts that there can be no just taxation without representation and the collective or representative consent of those to be taxed.

A DEFINING SYSTEM OF LAND TENURE

In England after the Norman Conquest, the operative legal principle of land tenure was that every acre of ground (as well as the surface area of lakes and streams) ultimately belonged to the king (the king's dominion). The legal formula for describing land tenure was the Latin equivalent of "A holds this land from B in the king's dominion." Landowners were said to hold title either mediately (with others standing between themselves and the king) or immediately (directly from the king). The king and the lords intervening between the landholder and the king all had at least theoretical rights in the same acreage to which the landholder laid claim and could require payment.

Feudal land tenure, or "holding in fee or fief," meant that the right to particular acreage was inheritable. The duty to perform services still might be attached to the land and could pass to heirs who never had dealt directly with the king or other intermediate overlord. The duties of feudal service might consist of military service, petty sergeanty (e.g., making arrows and knives), the duty to pay money rent or provide some other service; or for clerical holdings, the duty to pray for the souls of one or more of the overlords or his or their ancestors.

Of the various kinds of medieval tenancy, socage tenure evolved into a precursor of modern tenant/landlord relations. "Free socage" (or burgage in the towns) was defined as the residual category of tenures that did not fit any of the other categories. Typically this form of tenure required little more than paying nominal rents or performing nominal services (such as sending the overlord one rose or a basket of berries per year). In the first 200 years or so after the Norman Conquest, socage also could include the payment of substantial money rents or substantial services. (Among those listed are sending the overlord a sparrowhawk, a pair of gloves, or a pound of pepper each year, as well as a duty to plow the lord's lands for so many days per year).

Tenure in burgage, or ownership of land in a city or borough, was nearly identical to tenure in free socage. It typically involved nothing more than payment of money rent, with perhaps some duty of plowing included. Tenants of ancient boroughs (those that had borough status dating from before the Norman Conquest) typically performed no feudal services and paid only money rents.

Medieval English land tenure formally required ceremonies of homage and fealty, which were common throughout Europe. Homage is a ceremonial act that involves a symbolic subjection to one's overlord by placing one's hands within his and attesting faithfulness to him against all men except the king. Fealty is a loyalty oath that is sworn. It might be exacted as a condition of land tenure even if homage were not required. Originally, it apparently was intended to be performed at the close of the homage ceremony, but later practice seems to have been to require loyalty oaths (especially those in favor of the king) from every free male over the age of 12.

The ceremonies of homage and fealty created a somewhat one-sided relationship between lord and vassal. Although a lord forfeited his lordship by wrongly seizing a man's land or by failing to defend him, the law required that a man must bear with his lord's maltreatment of him for 30 days in war, for a year and a day in peace. Killing one's lord was high treason punishable by flaying alive, but a lord who killed his man was allowed to pay a monetary fine. At the same time, lords were required to warrant (protect) their tenants' tenures, defending them with force, if necessary. This is the origin of modern warranty deeds for land transfers.

The preservation of feudal land tenure after attempts to transfer holdings became problematic for the king and lords. The purchasers could be assumed not to wish to perform required feudal services. The statute *Quia emptores* of 1290 granted legal recognition to some sales and partial transfers such as leaseholds and life estates of land by all freemen, as long as the purchasers or other replacement tenants agreed to perform the same feudal services that their transferors were required to perform.

Property rights took another step forward in 1297. That year, Edward I was forced to concede to his barons that he had levied taxes without following the procedures set forth in Magna Carta in order to pay for his continued wars in France. Consequently, they forced him to confirm Magna Carta and the Charter of the Forests (*Carta de Foresta,* 1217), which Edward's father, Henry III, had confirmed in 1217, as a condition of any new tax levy. The Charter of the Forests extended many of the liberties and ancient customs to dwellers within the king's forest jurisdiction that had been extended to the population at large in Magna Carta.

In paragraph 1 of the Confirmation of the Charters of 1297, Edward explicitly allowed Magna Carta to be pleaded in the king's courts as "the common law" and the Forest Charter to be pleaded in the forest courts. Edward ordered that the two charters be sent to all the cathedral churches in the realm and to be read in public twice a year. Threats of excommunication also were to be read in the cathedrals before the people two times a year against those who "by word, deed, or counsel do contrary to the foresaid charters, or that in any point break or undo them." Finally, Edward promised that, except for remaining feudal duties, thereafter all "aids, tasks, and prises" (i.e., taxes) would be levied only with "the common consent of the realm, and for the common profit thereof." For the first time in English history, the king recognized that he could not levy new taxes unilaterally.

Earlier in the Summons of the Model Parliament of 1295, Edward established the principle that the entire kingdom (including the common people) was entitled to representation through the election of knights of the shires or counties (who later attended the parliament when it finally was summoned in 1297) in all deliberations on taxation. This constituted another significant step forward in the evolution of property rights because it was the first explicit recognition of the right of the freemen among the common people to parliamentary representation.

These charters of Edward I comprised the final step in preparing for the later growth and development of an elaborate system of property rights, which in turn gave rise to ideas about liberty itself.

3

The Birth of Modern Liberty

The English nobility drafted the constitutional documents of the 11th to 13th centuries. But a spirit of liberty began to spread among the rising middle classes as well, and in some instances it reached the lower classes, too. Most scholars agree that its evolution began during the reign of Edward III (1327-1377).

The first difficulties arose following the outbreak of the Hundred Years' War between England and France in 1337. In England, the war gave rise to continuing royal taxes (subject to parliamentary approval) to finance it. But bubonic/pneumonic plague – the Black Death – was the great catalyst of popular disaffection. The plague arrived in southwest England in August 1348 and died out in the northern counties by the spring of 1350. But its toll was astonishing. Approximately one-half of the English population died during this outbreak, while in an ordinary year perhaps one-twentieth would have died.

For the great landholders, the population decrease was catastrophic. While the demand for labor remained fairly constant, far fewer hands were available to perform it. The landlords, in turn, visited their catastrophe on their tenants, persuading the king to decree a wage-control act in 1349 that required laborers to demand no more than their accustomed wages, despite the labor shortage. (At the time, laborers typically earned one to two pence per day, the equivalent back then of two to five cents.)

This royal statute was reissued in 1351 with increased penalties for non-compliance, this time setting wage rates for various classes of laborers and requiring that all laborers swear twice a year that they would obey this law. Non-compliance, however, was general, and the real wage level rose to an estimated 50 percent above the 1348 rate during the 1350s. And in response to landlords' petitions, the statute was reenacted 13 times between 1357 and 1444.

During this period, a significant population of non-landowning and somewhat itinerant agricultural laborers arose. Because of the increase in agricultural wages, it became possible for the first time to earn an adequate living from agricultural labor without the burdens, feudal and otherwise, of landholding. In contrast, earlier generations of laborers had to hold at least some land in order to be able to feed themselves.

In 1377, Parliament voted to impose an annual head or poll tax on all laymen of four pence or the equivalent of two to four days' labor. This was a form of taxation previously unknown in England. The Church soon followed suit and imposed a similar tax on the clergy. Then in 1379, a graduated poll tax was imposed on all persons over 16 years of age, ranging from four pence for common laborers to four pounds for earls.

In May 1381, the common people began to revolt against the poll tax commissioners of the young king, Richard II. By the second week of June, there were simultaneous revolts in several parts of England, and rebels led by Wat Tyler entered London itself.

Tyler was killed inside London, and his followers were disarmed outside the city gates. The general revolt was then suppressed rapidly as nobles and gentlemen brought forth their own armed men to confront what had become a disorganized rabble. On June 24, 1381, a royal proclamation required all tenants to perform their accustomed services for their lords. On July 2, a royal proclamation revoked the manumission (liberation) promised by the king's charters issued to pacify the rebels while they were in London. Special courts were organized to hunt down, try, and execute the rebel leaders.

This uprising became known as the Peasants' Revolt of 1381, also called Wat Tyler's Rebellion. In its aftermath, in lieu of liberation of the serfs, landlords expanded the practice of commutation, or taking a money payment instead of enforcing the work requirement on manorial estates. The practical effect of this change was to give *villeins* (feudal serfs who owed services in exchange for land) nearly the same economic rights on the land as freehold tenants. Increasingly after that, the lords gave up enforcing the requirements of serfdom. By the middle of the 15th century, most of the English rural population was made up of free men who were no longer serfs. Instead of being attached to the land, these free people where ready to take the next step toward ownership and liberty. The impetus for that step was to come from an unlikely source: sheep.

ENCLOSURES

A rising demand for fine wool, typically produced from the merino sheep that were introduced into England from Spain in the late 15th and 16th centuries, caused landlords to calculate that more profit was to be made from raising sheep than growing grain. To provide adequate pasture, they began to enclose the tenant farmers' common fields (which were actually cultivated in narrow strips) with fences or hedgerows and to convert this land to pasture. Being unable to raise grain and pay money rents, the *villeins* and many small freeholders were evicted from manorial estates.

The first reported law cases in England that arose from evictions related to enclosures date from 1468 and 1484. They involved copyhold tenants—that is, tenants whose only claim to title was that they were entered on the service and rent rolls of the manor. This was the typical title status of the *villeins*. Copyhold tenancy meant that they were entitled to obtain a copy of the part of the roll on which they were entered to prove their customary status.

Originally, it was held that a copyhold tenant could *not* be evicted as long as he was considered a customary tenant and he tendered the required feudal service or money rent. But later, it became the common-law rule that ordinary copyhold tenants were tenants at the will of the landlord and could be evicted.

There were two great waves of enclosures in the British Isles, in the 16th century and again from the second half of the 18th century to the middle of the 19th century.

In the first wave, whole townships were emptied and filled with sheep and a few shepherds, and the political phenomenon of the rotten borough was created. (This was a borough or parliamentary district that had very few people in it but retained the same voting power as other boroughs with larger populations.) The enclosure movement further accelerated when King Henry VIII dissolved the monasteries in 1536. The monastic lands were sold or granted to new manorial lords who typically were more interested in enclosures and sheep-raising than in maintaining the ancient feudal forms of agriculture.

Commoners and nobility alike mounted protests against the enclosures and the evictions of the *villeins*. Sir Thomas More and other writers, especially in the later Elizabethan period, condemned the enclosures. Parliament enacted statutes against them (1488-1598) and created the first Corn Laws. These were intended to protect England's internal grain supply from diminution below what today would be called the national security level.

Regional popular uprisings against enclosures occurred between 1536 and 1552, by which time about one-half of the manors of England were enclosed. Parliament attempted to interfere directly in the property rights of manorial owners, at one point (1518) requiring a demonstration of public advantage before any enclosure could be enforced in the courts (not unlike the licensing or zoning laws common today). The *villeins* had public sympathy for their plight and the apparent weight of custom on their side, but the landlords had valid legal, economic, and customary arguments on their side also. Far fewer *villeins* than one might imagine had longstanding and unbroken customary links to particular plots of ground, largely because of the increasing mobility of feudal tenants since even before the Black Death years (1348-1350). Parliament finally repealed the first wave of enclosures in 1624.

The second wave of enclosures and clearances of tenant farmers in the British Isles in the 18th and early 19th centuries eventually reached the Scottish Highlands. Most of the remaining unenclosed English manors became enclosed within this time. This was accomplished through private acts of Parliament that permitted the enclosure of specifically designated lands. Small tenants who were thus evicted were offered modest cash compensation, but without land it became impossible to maintain the family milk cows and chickens that improved rural existence.

The private acts, which began in the early 18th century, accelerated in number and acreage covered after 1760. Eventually, a general Enclosure Act, largely replacing the private acts, was enacted in 1845 (amended in 1851).

In the early 19th century, the old forms of English agriculture—small-scale farming, using very little machinery for either grain-growing or raising animals—finally disappeared. They were overtaken by the combined onslaught of more modern and scientific farming, the enclosures, the rise of manufacturing employment for the working poor (or the frequent lack of such employment), the repeal of the Corn Laws (1846), and a financial panic in 1825 that bankrupted many rural borrowers.

The literary protest against this final wave of enclosures included Oliver Goldsmith's poem, "The Deserted Village" (1770), and William Cobbett's *Rural Rides* (1830). This time, however, there were no popular uprisings. In part this was because of a new option that did not exist in the 16th century—the possibility of emigration to America or, later, Australia.

As London grew, after the mid-19th century, the laws on enclosing public spaces changed. The courts initially followed a legal presumption in support of the right to enclose the commons, unless the public interest outweighed it. The courts later reversed their presumption in favor of preserving open spaces: There was no right to enclose the commons, unless the public interest required it. Thus was born the ancestor of modern zoning laws, from a movement to preserve the little that remained of the commons, but only after the last *villein* had been expelled.

THE FIRST MIDDLE-CLASS CONSTITUTION

The turmoil of England's 17th century, which saw a civil war, the beheading of a king, a revolution, and later, the restoration of the Stuart monarchy, also yielded a significant step forward in the development of property rights for the common man. As usual, the advance began with a fight over taxation.

Between 1629 and 1640, King Charles I convened no Parliaments. But he continued to collect three forms of tax—tonnage, poundage, and ship money—although the underlying statutory authorization for collection was unclear. Tonnage was a tax that merchants paid on both imports and exports, assessed at the rate of so much per ton. Poundage was a tax granted for the king's personal use of 12 pence (one shilling or roughly the equivalent back then of 25 cents) to the pound on all articles imported or exported, payable by both English and foreign merchants. Ship money was a special tax levied on residents of port cities and at other designated places for the fitting out of ships. These taxes were increasingly unpopular. In 1637, one of the Puritan leaders of the last Parliament, John Hampden, publicly refused to pay the ship money tax, for which he was tried. This event inflamed popular resentment of the king's imperious manner of governance.

Charles I called two Parliaments in 1640, a short one that lasted a month and another that sat for slightly more than 10 years (including two years after the king was dead, called the Rump Parliament. During this Long Parliament, the Puritan leaders made it clear that they would not authorize or renew the taxes that the king requested unless he submitted to their guidance. The king refused, and in 1642, the king himself led a band of armed men to Parliament to arrest five Puritan leaders of the House of Commons. Thus the First Civil War erupted between the king and Parliament. It would continue for nine years and include a campaign in Ireland.

One of the Puritan leaders, Oliver Cromwell, organized a new model army in which training and competence counted for more than peerage in leadership. In 1645, this Parliamentary army defeated the king's forces in the Battle of Naseby; afterward they had the king on the run. In the next two or three years, divisions of interest emerged in the House of Commons between the gentry (called the Presbyterians) and the middle class (for the most part, being middle class meant that people could both arm themselves and acquire a horse), who gravitated toward the party called the Independents. A Scottish army invaded England, and the king surrendered to that army in May 1646. However, the Scots promptly delivered him to Parliament (the Presbyterian faction).

In 1647, fearing a coalition of the nobles, the Presbyterians, and the king, Cromwell's army captured the king away from Parliament. Cromwell, originally an Independent, then moved toward the party of the Presbyterians. For a variety of reasons of high politics and intrigue, perhaps because they saw in the king a possible rallying point for the people, a prospect distasteful to the Presbyterians, the leaders of Parliament decided to try the king for treason (he had fought against Parliament, after all), and then to execute him. Charles I was beheaded January 30, 1649.

Developments leading to the execution added a chapter to the history of expanding liberty and property rights, traceable to the men in Cromwell's army. The Independents in the army were comprised of several not always cooperative factions. These included the Levellers. This name was a misnomer, given to them by their critics. The Levellers wanted equality of political rights for all free Englishmen, but they expressly abjured any interest in "leveling men's estates."

The Levellers' ideas were precursors to classical liberal thought. The comparatively modern notion that people have certain fundamental rights and liberties that no government can invade begins with them. The first time that one encounters the expression "fundamental right" is in writings associated with the Levellers and the English Civil War. From the Norman Conquest until the middle of the 17th century, the main premise of reformers always had been the restoration of the *ancient* rights and liberties of the people. After the middle of the 17th century, the reformers tended to demand the recognition of *fundamental* rights and liberties.

In their own era, the Levellers' ideas were taken up by the Agitators. These were representatives of the rank-and-file soldiers who were appointed by the

Independents to study and report to the regiments on political developments. The Agitators drafted pamphlets that were circulated throughout the army, and they also drafted petitions to Parliament.

The Agitators drafted the first version of a constitutional document *not* drafted by the nobility. That document, the Agreement of the People, was presented to the Army Council (headed by Cromwell) at Putney Church on October 29, 1647, and approved by the Council about one week later.

At this point, the king, whom the army was holding at Hampton Court, escaped (he was soon recaptured), and the army feared a Presbyterian plot in the king's escape. Meanwhile, the project of presenting an army petition to Parliament with the Agreement of the People attached went badly; the designated petitioners were arrested for sedition. During 1648, the Agitators drew up new petitions, including one with a demand for reopening "the late enclosures." That petition received 40,000 signatures, a vast number for that time. At the end of the year Independent grandees (senior officers) slightly modified a version of the Agreement. They presented it to Parliament the same day, January 20, 1649, that the king's treason trial commenced. The Agreement was lost in the parliamentary shuffling.

One of the most notable features of the final version of the Agreement was that the right to vote was extended only to "ratepayers and householders," while the earlier version extended the franchise to all freeholders and freemen, excepting only servants and beggars.

The Agreement also included sections of great significance to the development of property rights and liberty over the next 150 years. The paragraphs forbidding Parliament from making laws in areas affecting fundamental and natural rights were a beacon light for America's Founding Fathers—both those who were apostles of the Enlightenment, with its emphasis on natural law (such as Jefferson), and those who were defenders of the traditions of English liberty (such as Adams).

The enumerated fundamental rights in the Agreement included freedom from military conscription for service in foreign wars, full faith and credit (the guarantee of the taxing power) to support payment of public obligations, equal protection of the laws, a prohibition of ex post facto laws, a prohibition of the leveling of estates or the destruction or communization of property (which some were advocating), a prohibition of compulsory religious observance, and the free exercise of religion (except for Catholics and Anglicans). For the first time in a constitutional document, it became clear that one's religious views might affect one's civil liberties. All these issues would be addressed explicitly in the American Constitution.

The principal significance of the Agreement of the People for modern readers is that it is the first constitutional document enumerating the "fundamental rights of free Englishmen" and spelling out those rights with sufficient clarity to enable them to be implemented. Preservation of property rights, both real and financial, is one of those fundamental rights. Unfortunately, it required another 40 years of struggle before Parliament actually both adopted and generally began to conduct state affairs in reasonable compliance with such a fundamental constitutional document. In 1689, the Crown and Parliament would finally recognize a free man's fundamental rights—the essential demand of the Levellers in the Agreement of the People—in the English Declaration of Rights. But in 1649, the struggle for this recognition experienced significant setbacks.

After the king's execution, England was ruled by the Rump Parliament and a Council of State appointed by it. The Levellers published new pamphlets critical of this Council. In response, the Leveller leaders were charged with treason and arrested. Although the army that Cromwell had raised and trained attempted to remain together and was still camped near London (as a political force to be reckoned with until the Independents' demands were dealt with), it became divided after the king's execution. With a modest use of force by the grandees, the army was disbanded.

The imprisoned Leveller leaders were put on trial in 1649. Interestingly, proving the value of trial by jury, the first leader to be tried, John Lilburne, argued so persuasively to the jury that he was acquitted. The others awaiting trial were not tried. But afterward the force of the Leveller's faction, with its emphasis on political rights for all free men, was spent.

By 1653, Cromwell made himself Lord Protector of England, in effect a military dictator. He died five years later. In 1660, after a brief protectorate under Cromwell's son Richard, who resigned, King Charles II (1630-1685), son of Charles I, was given the throne, marking the Restoration of the Stuart monarchy.

4

The Philosophers of Freedom

In the 17th century, free Englishmen learned that property rights and individual liberty necessarily march hand in hand and that one cannot with surety have the one without the other. By mid-century, this essential connection began to be articulated by two great moral philosophers, Thomas Hobbes (1588-1679) and John Locke (1632-1704).

Although diametrically opposed on the role of government, both of these Englishmen described protection of property rights as the chief goal of society. The difference was how they said society should achieve this. Hobbes favored a strong government that had a monopoly on the use of force to defend the right to property. Without the strength of a central state, he wrote, society would devolve into anarchy.

Locke held that individual property rights precede the claims of government. Individuals earn these rights through their labor and are entitled to defend their property through individual use of force. For Locke, protecting property was more than a primary goal of society. It was a fundamental component of liberty. In Locke's view, property rights and personal liberty either marched hand in hand or not at all.

The tension between the theories of Hobbes and Locke continue to this day and find expression in current disputes about eminent domain, zoning, and inheritance taxes.

THOMAS HOBBES

By the age of 20, the precocious and brilliant Thomas Hobbes was working as a tutor to royalty. In this capacity, he made several tours to France, Italy, and Germany, where he met with leading thinkers such as Galileo and Descartes.

He also began to write about philosophy, science, and mathematics.

In his writings on government, he defended the absolute power of the royal state as being necessary to keep humans from falling into a "natural" state of war with each other. When the English Civil War began in 1642, Hobbes, fearing arrest or worse from those who opposed the king, fled to Paris. There, among other things, he was the mathematics tutor for the future King Charles II, who was also living in exile.

When first examined, Hobbes's ideas might strike modern sensibilities as either immoral or amoral because they often seem to denigrate the idea of a beneficent, natural justice in the world. Hobbes believed that nature was, at best, a neutral factor in men's lives and that it often was hostile and cruel.

In fact, Hobbes was a proponent of the material progress of mankind, and his views have an underlying moral sense about them. But living in the turbulence of 17th-century England, it was only natural that he should point out that material progress is difficult to achieve. He believed that the strong arm of the prince, sword ever at the ready, was necessary to insure the progress and comparative happiness of the people.

Given this, it is understandable that Hobbes would endorse taxes to support the sword-bearer and other governmental interference in an individual's property rights as a fair price to pay for the safety that a strong government could guarantee.

Hobbes's best-known work was *Leviathan* (1651). The following points of his philosophy, related to sovereignty, property rights, and taxation, are among the most famous.

Labor is the basic commodity (we would say factor of production) that creates wealth. Even small territories such as city states have become rich through manufacturing and trade, both of which depend on labor.

The distribution within a society of the means of a person's sustenance depends on divisions of material goods into legal categories such as mine and yours and his. Those categories are regulated in every state by the *sovereign* power. In the absence of state power, there is "a perpetual war of every man against his neighbor." In such an anarchic situation, force alone determines the distribution of property. The institution of property thus depends on an effective sovereign power to make the laws. The main concern of the law is the *distribution* of property, a form of justice (in Greek, *nomos*).

In property distributions, the sovereign should assign every man his portion, not according to any plan made by the subjects. In the case of conquest, the conquered hold their property titles from the conqueror and not by any prior right.

The basic property right is the right to exclude all other persons from the use of property, but not to exclude the sovereign, whether it is an assembly or a monarch. Sovereign monarchs or assemblies should not be criticized because the subjects have authorized their actions by bestowing the sovereign power in the first place. The sovereign has the right to regulate all domestic and foreign commerce.

Taxation by the sovereign is merely the wage due to those who hold the public sword for defending private men in the exercise of their trades and professions. Equal taxation should be imposed on consumption.

Charity may take care of the incapacitated, but the able-bodied should be required to work. To provide demand for labor, laws should encourage occupations using a great deal of labor. As the numbers of the able-bodied poor increase, they should be transplanted into under-inhabited countries. They should not exterminate the aborigines found there, but the natives may be constrained to live more closely together and to adopt settled agriculture. When the world becomes overpopulated, the "last remedy" is war, "which provides for every man, by Victory, or Death."

The sovereign has a duty to make good laws. All laws made by the sovereign are necessarily just. The general nature of the sovereign's regulatory laws should be like rules of traffic for the conduct of commerce. A good law is one that is necessary for the good of the people. Its reasoning and purpose should be clear from the face of the statute. (Currently, very few statutes would qualify as good laws using Hobbes's definition.)

There are a number of resonances between the *Leviathan* and the writings of later generations of political economists and lawgivers. Some writers, such as the young John Adams, Thomas Jefferson, and George Mason, wrote in reaction against Hobbes's ideas. No Founding Father of 1776, for example, would have agreed with much of Hobbes's depiction of what the *lawful* powers of the sovereign include. Others affirmed Hobbes's views. For example, Treasury Secretary Alexander Hamilton, Chief Justice John Marshall, Senator and Secretary of State Henry Clay, and President Theodore Roosevelt probably would have agreed with most or all of the above points excerpted from Hobbes. They all advocated a strong and vigorous executive branch and the centralization of governmental power. Some, including Marshall, Clay, and Roosevelt, actively encouraged foreign colonizing efforts.

33

Hobbes defended Stuart absolutism, the vesting of absolute power in the ruler. But he cannot be ignored, even if no one is an absolute monarchist today, because of the undisputed influence of his ideas on those who advocate a strong and active governmental role in the management of property rights.

THE ENGLISH DECLARATION OF RIGHT AND BILL OF RIGHTS

Twenty-five years after the restoration of the Stuart monarchy, James II took the throne. Three years later, in 1688, Great Britain again prepared for civil war. The central reasons involved disagreement over the roles of Parliament and the king, the establishment of the Protestant vs. the Catholic religion, and the king's power to borrow money and impose taxes for purposes lacking parliamentary consent.

James was a practicing Catholic and was always mistrusted by the mostly Protestant Parliament. In Parliament's eyes, he seemed constantly to be scheming with Louis XIV of France against the liberties of the Protestants of the Netherlands. This was so even though James had consented to give his daughter Mary in marriage to his nephew, the Protestant Prince William of Orange, the ruler of Holland. In domestic policy, James offended important sectors of the Protestant clergy by a series of proclamations aimed at restoring equality of civil rights and public religious observance to English Catholics.

In late 1688, James and a small army confronted William of Orange on the coast of England. Deserted by those around him, including many of his own soldiers, James agreed to vacate the throne. Soon afterward, he fled, first to France and then to Ireland. There he raised a Catholic army to confront son-in-law William and a Protestant army. On July 1, 1690, William of Orange (popularly known as King Billy) defeated James II in the Battle of the Boyne. This victory is still commemorated every year by Protestants in Northern Ireland in parades that have become another flashpoint in the sectarian conflict there.

Upon losing the Battle of the Boyne, James retired to France, although his endeavors to return to the English throne persisted until a formal peace treaty was signed in 1697. The Glorious Revolution of 1688-89 that led to his deposition is often called the Bloodless Revolution, because armed conflict was generally avoided in England. But it was far from bloodless for the Irish.

When William and Mary ascended the throne in 1689, they had to accept certain provisions set by Parliament as a condition of becoming rulers. These were spelled out in two documents that became milestones in British constitutional history.

The Declaration of Right was approved in August 1689. With two amendments, it was enacted October 25, 1689, as the Bill of Rights. This put fundamental principles of the English Constitution into statutory form. By accepting its provisions, William and Mary agreed that the monarchy would be subject to Parliament in all matters of lawmaking.

The Declaration and Magna Carta were the English constitutional documents most widely known to the generation of our own Founding Fathers. The Declaration clearly influenced later American constitutional documents. Its form—a preamble followed by a recital of grievances or public indictment, recapitulation, and petition or declaration—is echoed in our Declaration of Independence.

In one section entitled the Heads of Grievances, the Declaration of Right accused the king of having subverted the Protestant religion and the laws and liberties of the kingdom in the following ways, among others:

By suspending laws without the consent of Parliament and by raising taxes by pretended "royal prerogative."

By keeping a domestic standing army in time of peace and quartering soldiers contrary to law.

By disarming Protestants while letting Catholics go armed.

By requiring excessive bail, imposing excessive fines, and inflicting illegal and cruel punishments.

All of these issues affected the future course of Anglo-American property rights as well as political liberty.

Another section of the Declaration of Right, called the Declaration, said that the practices complained of were illegal. In another noteworthy section, Parliament petitioned the king and queen to declare that the rights and liberties asserted and claimed in the larger document were "the true, ancient, and indubitable rights and liberties of the people of this kingdom," and that the royal officers and ministers and their successors always should strictly hold and observe those rights and liberties "for all times to come."

The inclusion of the word "indubitable" is a critical feature of the English Declaration. The language that described what reformers wanted formally changed. (For our purposes, reformers were advocates of more widely distributed and more thoroughly established property rights.) The ancient rights still existed and still were important, but within 100 years of the Declaration of Right, all references to the ancient rights came to be subsumed into the demand for recognition of fundamental rights.

The property-protecting provisions of the English Declaration of Right inspired George Mason's draft of the Virginia Declaration of Rights in 1776. This in turn reflected the spirit of the times, in Virginia at least, that further inspired Thomas Jefferson's draft of the Declaration of Independence, which was written one month after the Virginia document. This spirit, already evident in 1689, eventually led to the apogee of classical liberal thought and its liberation of the human spirit a century later: the period that included the American Revolution, the framing of the U.S. Constitution, and the early years of the French Revolution.

JOHN LOCKE

The modern, mainstream path of *classically liberal* thought on property rights is largely derived from thinkers such as John Locke as well as from political activists such as the Levellers. They were reacting, on the basis of similar sets of political events, *against* the ideal of a powerful and centralized governmental authority that Hobbes advocated.

Locke was the last, and unquestionably the single greatest, economic and philosophical influence of the 17th century on the ideas of the generation of the American Founding Fathers about property rights. Educated at Christ Church College, Oxford, he studied medicine and became the personal physician to the Earl of Shaftesbury. Through the Earl's influence, he made several trips abroad and drafted constitutions for the colonies of North and South Carolina. He also became secretary to the Council of Trade and Plantations in London (later known as the Board of Trade, it was roughly equivalent to the U.S. Department of Commerce). Through these endeavors, he acquired some practical business and economic experience that later came to influence his philosophical writings. (In contrast, Hobbes had no practical experience.)

Locke identified with the Protestant political factions that were losing influence in the last years of the Stuart kings. As a result, he lived in Holland from 1684 until the abdication of James II in 1688. In 1689 and 1690, after the Glorious Revolution that restored the Protestants to power, he finally published his two *Treatises of Civil Government,* written years earlier.

In the *First Treatise,* Locke refuted arguments for the divine right of kings. In the *Second Treatise of Civil Government* (also called *Concerning Civil Govern-*

ment: Second Essay), he outlined his theory of good government. In a preface, Locke indicated that the two essays, although having been written earlier, were meant to vindicate the Glorious Revolution and the accession of William III to the throne. In stark contrast to Hobbes, he argued that the people had a natural right to depose any king who abused their ancient and natural liberties.

Locke wrote in his *Second Essay* that "every man has a 'property' in his own 'person'" and "nobody has any right to [this] but himself." He also described how the simple labor of gathering acorns in a common forest imparts to them the distinct character of property. If a man boiled them and prepared a soup from them and then derived nourishment from them, no one could question seriously whether the acorns properly were his own or someone else's.

Locke assumed that, in a state of nature, all men could take from the commons whatever was necessary for their sustenance, as long as a sufficient quantity of equally good things remained for others to take. He said that a man's labor transforms natural or common things into property. This became a foundation for later philosophical and economic theories of value based on labor.

The consent of others is unnecessary for the taking of sustenance from the commons, he claimed. However, no one is allowed to remove from the commons more than "any one can make use of to any advantage of life before it spoils. . . . Whatever is beyond this is more than [a man's] . . . share, and belongs to others. Nothing was made by God for man to spoil or destroy."

Applying this labor principle to real property, Locke argued that it, too, is acquired in the same manner as personal property: by labor. "As much land as a man tills, plants, improves, cultivates, and can use the product of, so much is his property. He by his labor does, as it were, enclose it from the common." A man's labor on land bars others from staking an equal claim to it. No one is harmed by such "enclosures from the commons" as long as it doesn't deprive others of appropriate enclosures for themselves. He continues:

> God gave the world to men in common, but since He gave it them for their benefit and the greatest conveniencies of life they were capable to draw from it, it cannot be supposed He meant it should always remain common and uncultivated. He gave it to the use of the industrious and rational (and labour was to be his title to it); not to the fancy or covetousness of the quarrelsome and contentious. He that had as good left for his improvement as was already taken up needed not complain, ought not to meddle with what was already improved by another's labour.

At the time Locke was writing, one-half of the English commons already was enclosed. On the enclosures, he made the following points with clear relevance to property rights:

> In England and other countries with sufficiently advanced economies, any enclosure from the commons requires the common consent of the other citizens of the relevant jurisdiction. All mankind does not share in the common property of particular countries or localities—the local residents should control decisions regarding disposition of common property.
>
> God's original command to man was to appropriate and subdue the earth. Man's wants or needs forced him to engage in labor. Labor, in turn, gave man title to property on which he had expended labor. The command to subdue and the need to labor each give title to the other.
>
> Work on the materials of man's life introduces the concept of private possessions. However, it is not until the concept of money, a non-depreciating store of value, is introduced in a society that a man can control more possessions than he can make direct use of profitably.

Steps

Locke points out that location matters in real estate: An acre of good wheat land in England might be worth a thousand times the value of a comparable acre in the wild America of that day. The difference, Locke said, would be in part because of the economies of scale that the division of labor in England permits, contrasted with the solo actor and largely subsistence farmers on the frontier of America. He also noted that large tracts of waste land are unlikely to occur in countries "that have consented to the use of money."

Perishable goods, he wrote, constitute the bulk of the things most useful to the life of man. In rude societies such as the America of that day, gold, silver, and diamonds would be accounted of less practical use than acorns, apples, and sheep. Once some durable thing comes into use as a form of money, a man "might heap up as much of these durable things as he pleased" without worry about physical decay, "the exceeding of the bounds of his just property not lying in the largeness of his possession, but the perishing of anything uselessly in it."

Essentially, Locke argued, a man's right to particular property and his own convenience "went together." A man's title was clear for the things on which he had expended his own labor, and the products of that labor easily could be seen by all; but "it was useless, as well as dishonest, to carve himself too much, or take more than he needed." The moral wrong consisted of taking things on which one had not expended one's own labor.

Later in the *Second Essay*, Locke observed that the principal objective of civil society is to preserve a man's "Property, that is, his Life, Liberty and Estate, against the Injuries and Attempts of other Men...." Good government, he added, as much as possible makes laws to preserve the property of all members of a society.

In Locke's system, the legislature, not the executive, is the chief power in government. The principal objective of this government, and the ultimate reason why men enter into society instead of fending for themselves, is the preservation of property. Locke rejects the idea, espoused by Hobbes and other defenders of the state-centered theory of property rights, that men lose their absolute title to property by entering into society (or in Hobbes's case, by subjecting themselves to the sovereign).

Locke wrote that a government that pretends to have the power to take the whole *or any part* of a man's property, in effect leaves that man with no property at all. Such a man necessarily has to hold his property title at the sufferance of the powerful, and not from any right of his own. Locke notes that, even in the military, where commanders might have power of life and death over their men, they may not command a soldier to give them even a single penny. Commanders enjoy their power for the preservation of the rest of society, but that power does not extend to disposing of a man's property.

No taking of property can occur without a man's own consent. As a bulwark against the temptation of inappropriate property takings by the state, Locke recommends that legislatures be composed of "variable assemblies" of people who, upon leaving office, once again are as subject to the common laws as everyone else. In systems where the legislature sits permanently or for a long time, or where rule is concentrated in one man, as in absolute monarchies, the danger arises that the holders of power will begin to think of themselves as having a separate and distinct interest from the rest of the community. In such cases, Locke writes, the governing class "will be apt to increase their own Riches and Power, by taking, what they think fit, from the People."

The generation of America's Founding Fathers was in nearly complete agreement with this point.

Locke expounds on taxation as follows: No one should be taxed without his own consent, the consent of the majority, or the consent of their duly selected representatives. Anyone who claims authority to tax by his own decree "invades the *Fundamental Law of Property*, and subverts the end of Government. For what property have I in that which another may by right take, when he pleases to himself?" Daniel Webster, acting as an attorney, later made a variation of the same argument, which Chief Justice John Marshall then repeated in the Supreme Court's opinion in *McCulloch v. Maryland* (1819): The power to tax involves the power to destroy.

Locke also wrote that legitimate lawgivers should be as free of the taint of corruption in lawmaking as possible. He articulates the *non-delegation doctrine*, which holds that the governing body to which a particular power is delegated by the people cannot lawfully transfer that power away from itself. This is a concept frequently violated in modern practice. Since the U.S. Supreme Court decided *J.W. Hampton v. United States* (1928), for example, the last decision upholding non-delegation doctrine, the Court usually allows the permanent delegation to the executive branch (or to agencies accountable to the executive branch) of powers explicitly delegated in the Constitution to Congress alone. The Office of the U.S. Trade Representative (trade agreements) and the Treasury's Exchange Stabilization Fund (foreign exchange market interventions) both are executive branch agencies created in 1934 to engage in activities originally confided to Congress alone under the commerce clause and the coining money clause, respectively, of Article I .

Locke invokes natural law as the ultimate sanction for his proposed scheme of government. He reminds those who govern that they exercise a trust "put in them by the Society, and the Law of God and Nature."

He closes the *Second Essay* with four main recommendations. The first is that those who govern do so "by promulgated establish'd Laws," which means that there should be no secret laws and that the laws should be duly enacted by established procedure. Every man also should be equal before the law—the law should not play favorites.

The second is that laws also should have no other aim but the ultimate good of the people. (Even Thomas Hobbes could have agreed on that objective.) Thirdly, taxation should be decided upon only by the people directly or by their duly elected representatives. Finally, the non-delegation doctrine must be respected.

In the final paragraphs of the *Second Essay*, Locke makes the main points about distributions of power within government and between the government and the people. Those ideas influenced, among others, George Mason of Virginia, principal draftsman of the Virginia Declaration of Rights in May 1776, and George Wythe, also of Virginia, a famous law teacher and the instructor of both Thomas Jefferson and future Chief Justice John Marshall. It is through this vein that the ideas of John Locke came to have the great influence that they did on the generation of our Founding Fathers.

Locke's theories of property rights were carried forward in the next generation through the writings of the Englishmen John Trenchard and Thomas Gordon in *The Independent Whig* and *Cato's Letters* (1719-1723). These latter essays were widely read in Colonial America. By this route, Locke's ideas also became the bedrock doctrine of property rights reflected in the 18th century English, Scottish, and French Enlightenments. Locke's disciples included more or less everyone later considered to be in the classical liberal Pantheon a century after he died.

5

Enlightenment in America

No single book or pamphlet electrified American public opinion in favor of independence as much as Thomas Paine's *Common Sense,* published in early 1776. In it, the British-born firebrand lays out in plain language the argument against both hereditary government and the English rule of America and for independence and representative democracy.

But the ground in which Paine's pamphlet flourished was prepared nearly a century earlier, with the publication of John Locke's treatises, and a half-century after that by a series of essays on the natural rights of free Englishmen published in London by John Trenchard and Thomas Gordon in *The Independent Whig* and *Cato's Letters* (1719-1723). Every influential American read Trenchard and Gordon, even a generation or two afterward among the educated classes.

Trenchard and Gordon began publishing *The Independent Whig* to "attack High Church pretensions and, more generally, the establishment of religion." They began *Cato's Letters* to attack corruption, both petty and grand, in English high society and government in the aftermath of the South Sea Bubble, a great stock market boom-and-bust that involved political corruption.

John Adams and his friend Josiah Quincy, Jr., both read and admired the constitutional precepts taught by Trenchard and Gordon. Benjamin Franklin, who had helped Thomas Paine emigrate to Philadelphia, republished them. John Dickinson (who was both a member of the Continental Congress from Pennsylvania and a signer of the Constitution from Delaware) quoted from them.

The Americans' view of taxation by London descended from the thinking of these radical Whigs. Their well-known argument was that particular forms of taxation, such as stamps on legal documents and tea taxes, were not inherently objectionable. Rather they objected to the principle of taxation without representation in Parliament. Driven by the new forms of taxation as well as by new methods of enforcement, such as searches of homes and warehouses for contraband or untaxed items, a new notion began to take hold in the colonies: independence from England.

It appeared in New England as early as 1761, in the wake of the *Writs of Assistance* case that John Adams helped make famous. This case involved British customs officers requiring local law enforcement officials to assist them in searches of private houses and stores. And it probably is the main source of the Fourth Amendment of the U.S. Constitution, which prohibits unreasonable searches and seizures and stands as one of the principal bulwarks of the classical liberal understanding of property rights in the Constitution.

Support for independence also took root in Virginia and several of the Middle Atlantic colonies during the 1760s. The general source of colonial dissatisfaction during this time was the series of new British taxes imposed from London following the close of the Seven Years' War (known in America as the French and Indian War) in 1763.

The fiery Boston lawyer James Otis Jr. led Colonial protests that caused the 1766 repeal of two tax acts. The Revenue Act of 1764 levied a sugar tax of three pence (or the equivalent back then of seven cents) per gallon of molasses. The Stamp Act of 1765 imposed a tax on legal documents, newspapers, playing cards, and other papers. Otis next organized protests against the Townshend Act of 1767, which replaced the Stamp Act. He argued that as long as Americans were unrepresented in Parliament, Parliament had no right to tax them and that such taxes were a threat to the natural rights of free Englishmen. In the pre-Revolutionary War period, American protesters believed that if they ever conceded the legitimacy of direct taxation while they were not represented in Parliament, none of their property rights could be viewed as secure.

In 1774, opposition in the Colonies mounted because of the Intolerable Acts directed against Massachusetts that Parliament passed following the Boston Tea Party. The Intolerable Acts included closing the port of Boston and replacing the upper house of the state legislature with direct appointees of the Crown. By late 1774, British General Thomas Gage was fortifying Boston, and country people throughout the Colonies were organizing militias to operate against British forces.

The first military skirmishes, on April 19, 1775, began when General

Gage's forces attempted to seize an armory of militia weapons and ammunition in Concord, Massachusetts. So began the American Revolution, with what Emerson 60 years later called "the shot heard round the world" at the Battle of Lexington and Concord. Two months after the skirmish, English and American forces met at Breed's Hill (wrongly called Bunker Hill) in Charlestown, Massachusetts, in the first major military encounter of the war. The British won that bloody confrontation, but with great cost of officers and men killed and wounded.

That same month, June 1775, John Adams persuaded the Continental Congress, a new body appointed by the states in 1774, to designate George Washington of Virginia as general and commander-in-chief of continental forces in Massachusetts. Washington left Congress to drive British troops from Boston, which he succeeded in doing over the course of the following winter. His success was insured by artillery support provided by General Henry Knox. Knox used cannons transported overland in mid-winter from Fort Ticonderoga on the New York-Vermont border to bombard British-occupied Boston from Roxbury Heights. Within a day, British General William Howe, who succeeded General Gage in command, agreed to evacuate the city on March 17, 1776. March 17 still is celebrated as a public holiday in Boston (Evacuation Day), but it also is St. Patrick's Day, which might explain the enthusiasm with which the holiday is celebrated in Boston.

COLONIAL CHARTERS AND INDEPENDENCE

By the time of independence, all but 4 of the 13 colonies had either royal provincial charters or direct royal government, culminating a process of conversion of earlier charters that began in 1691 with the new charter for Massachusetts. The royal colonies had home rule for most purposes, but they also had royal governors, were subject to British navigation and customs acts, and implicitly were subject to British taxation, at least in the eyes of London.

These charters had an impact on early legal theories about corporate property rights because they decreed, ultimately, that land title decisions would be made in London. Americans, however, were imbued with common-law and Lockean ideas that the first "civilized" person to claim and perform labor on a parcel of land gained title to it. They eventually objected to London's role in assigning titles and, during the period preceding Independence, demanded local determination of legal and commercial affairs.

Early colonial charters took one of three forms. Joint-stock charters and proprietary charters were designed with commercial objectives in mind. Their purpose was to make money either for shareholders in the case of joint-stock charters, or individuals or families in the case of proprietary charters. Religious charters were designed to allow the formation of religious communities.

Both religious charters, such as the Massachusetts Bay Company charter, and the early commercial charters, such as the Virginia Company, could be interpreted as allowing for a degree of self-determination dependent on the physical location of the charter. The people holding the charters could make the rules. Not so with royal charters. These gave the Crown the right to appoint colonial governors and to give final approval of colonial laws.

The first significant colonial charter that lasted was a joint-stock trading company charter issued to the Virginia Company in 1606. Initially, King James I retained the right of governing the charter company colonies. But by 1612, Virginia was issued a new charter requiring the company's shareholders (not necessarily representatives of the colonists) to meet in London quarterly in "great and general courts" to make ordinances for the colony that were no longer subject to direct rule by royal agents.

The first significant royal charter that lasted was granted in 1620 to the Council for New England for settlements north of Virginia. It founded its only successful colony, the Plymouth Plantation, that same year in Massachusetts.

The Council later founded fishing settlements in Dorchester and Cape Ann (modern Gloucester). In 1629, the Dorchester colonists obtained a royal charter for a colony along the lines of the revised Virginia Company charter of 1612, which conflicted with the charter for the new Massachusetts Bay Company (also issued in 1629). Both corporations' charters and governing courts were still in England.

The Massachusetts Bay Company's shareholders fell into two main groups: Puritan separatists and London merchants interested primarily in trade. When John Winthrop, leader of the separatists, emigrated in 1630, he brought the Company charter with him. This symbolic act enabled the colonists to claim that they now had the right to govern themselves in America without reference to a court of shareholders or directors in London.

The Massachusetts Bay Colony was organized along the lines of a theocracy. Only church members in good standing with the Puritan hierarchy were allowed to vote or own property. This was an issue until the charter was revoked in 1684, and the colony was united with Plymouth Plantation under a new royal charter in 1691.

For proprietary charters, the Crown granted English aristocrats the right to establish feudal estates in the New World. Charter holders would retain most of the legal attributes of land ownership and rent land to tenants. If the feudal overlords wished, they could require tenants to perform feudal service such as plowing fields or serving in the manor house. The Council for New England began with a proprietary charter but surrendered it after 15 years when no permanent colony outside Plymouth was founded. Nova Scotia was a proprietary grant to Sir William Alexander in 1621. Lord Calvert obtained a proprietary grant in part of Newfoundland in 1623.

The failure of Calvert's colony led to the issuance of a new proprietary grant to him for the Maryland colony in 1632. Calvert was required, however, to make laws and impose taxes (as distinguished from land rents) "only with the consent of the freemen resident" in his new colony.

All new English colonies in North America after 1660 were founded under similar proprietary charters. New York was a pre-existing Dutch proprietary colony started by the Dutch West India Company. The English captured New York in 1664, and the New York and New Jersey colonies were given to the Duke of York (later King James II). The Carolinas were given as proprietary colonies to friends of King Charles II in 1660. Georgia was chartered as a proprietary colony in 1732 for 20 years, after which title was to revert to the king.

William Penn obtained a proprietary grant, intended as a settlement for Quakers and other religious dissenters, for what later became Pennsylvania and Delaware, starting in 1681. Penn's grant also made it clear that the Crown intended to exercise a more direct role in colonial governance, even in the proprietary colonies.

The British government began to convert earlier colonial charters to royal provincial charters or direct royal government in 1691, beginning with Massachusetts Bay, and the franchise or right to vote was extended to non-members of the Puritan church.

By the period 1776-1781, only two joint-stock trading corporation charters (Connecticut and Rhode Island) and two proprietary colonies (Pennsylvania and Maryland) remained. All the rest were royal colonies. In early 1776, the Continental Congress recommended that the states begin to prepare new constitutions because, as a matter of law, the old royal charters would become ineffective once independence was declared.

THE VIRGINIA DECLARATION OF RIGHTS

The Virginia Declaration of Rights was drafted as part of a project for a state constitution that would replace Virginia's royal charter. Approved on June 12, 1776, around a month before the Declaration of Independence, it was at the time the most important constitutional declaration in the English language since the Glorious Revolution of 1688. Among other things, the Virginia Declaration provided the most thorough listing of property rights found in any English-language constitutional document since Magna Carta. It also was widely used as a model for other state declarations and became the basis for the U.S. Constitution's Bill of Rights.

The Declaration is the gold standard of 18th-century classical liberal ideals, having been shaped by learned and devout followers of John Locke's political theory.

It was written by George Mason (1725-1792), a former Virginia judge and a plantation-owning neighbor of George Washington on the Potomac River. Although Mason is one of the least known among the older generation of American revolutionaries, he was one of its most important figures. With the possible exception of George Wythe (1726-1807), who was the law teacher of both Thomas Jefferson and John Marshall, Mason is regarded generally as the most learned and influential person from his generation in the history of Anglo-American liberties and property rights.

In addition to writing Virginia's Declaration of Rights, he was a delegate to the Constitutional Convention in Philadelphia. He objected to ratification of the Constitution because of the undue concentration of central federal power that he discerned there. His objections eventually led to the addition of the first 10 amendments, the Bill of Rights, in 1791.

Mason's Declaration emphasizes the natural equality and independence of men and their inherent and unalienable rights, which the Declaration names. Chief among these is pursuing and obtaining happiness and safety and the enjoyment of life and liberty, including specifically the means of acquiring and possessing property.

Property rights are directly addressed in two key clauses. One states that taxation or public takings of private property should be prohibited without an individual's consent or the consent of elected representatives. Another specifies that customary 12-person juries should be preserved in trials involving property or personal injuries.

Other features that would soon become critical aspects of the fledgling American republic also impacted property rights because they guarded against too-strong governmental control over individual lives. The Virginia Declaration specifies that public office should not be inherited; that executive, legislative, and judicial powers should be separated; and that elections should be free of special taxes, with universal suffrage. And because since at least the time of the Roman Empire, military service had been a determining factor for land ownership, the Declaration held that a well-regulated militia composed of the people "trained to arms" is required for the defense of a free state.

The Declaration also stated that standing armies in peacetime are to be avoided as dangerous to liberty. Perhaps most importantly, the Declaration held that the military is to be subordinated to civilian power; and that "a firm adherence to justice, moderation, temperance, frugality and virtue, and . . . a frequent recurrence to fundamental principles" are required to sustain free government and the "blessing of liberty."

Finally, the Virginia Declaration states that all men are "entitled to the free exercise of religion, according to the dictates of conscience." This religious freedom also meant that members of no single faith would have the exclusive right to own property or the right to exclude non-adherents from property ownership.

The Preamble of the Virginia Declaration clarifies that the right of constitution-making belongs to the people at large *and to their posterity*, not to one or more classes or sets of persons separated from the people, and not to one generation exclusively. In contrast, in both medieval England and pre-revolutionary France, the concurrence of all three estates or classes of the people (the nobles or bishops of the church, the secular nobles, and the freemen among the common people or the Third Estate) was required to change the constitutional frame of government.

The Virginians also made it clear that the rights described belong to posterity as well as to any present generation—that is, no one should have the right to bind future generations to a harmful agreement or arrangement in derogation of fundamental rights.

The Virginians' legacy on this point was a general notion that each current generation should have at least one chance to change the form of government. As expressed in modern state constitutions, a call for a new constitutional convention is required to be placed on the ballot once every 20 years or so.

WHY CONSTITUTIONS MATTER

The idea that certain rights are fundamental was, by the time Mason was writing, clearly an established Anglo-American notion. But modern debate over the nature of fundamental rights tends to ignore the progressive evolution of ideas that lead up to the Constitution and The Bill of Rights.

There is a classical legacy of fundamental rights that later generations may dispute or alter, in the duly established manner provided by law, but the Virginians were very clear that only a wicked person would want to retract the fundamental rights that they identified in Mason's Declaration.

Mason, Jefferson, Madison, and other classical liberals argued that a large set of natural rights was implicit both in the Virginia Declaration and the modern state and federal constitutions that followed.

Others disagreed. These included Alexander Hamilton, John Adams (after he returned from England in 1788), John Marshall, and the Federalist Party that emerged during George Washington's second term as president. These statesmen argued against recognizing any fundamental right or protection from governmental interference that is neither enumerated specifically in the constitution, nor logically derived from enumerated fundamental rights or liberties by necessary and unavoidable implication.

Richard A. Posner, a federal appellate judge as well as a noted law teacher and author, offers a modern and moderate view of the debate about fundamental rights that essentially splits the difference between the two camps. In his *Economic Analysis of Law* (Aspen Publishers, Seventh Edition, 2007), he describes various modern economic theories of constitutions and defines the economic basis of a constitution as "a type of legislation that (1) requires a supermajority to change and (2) sets forth the fundamental powers, duties, and structure of the government."

Posner basically understands and acknowledges the presumptive (or at least the historically claimed) moral superiority of classical liberal approaches to, for example, problems of property rights. But he prefers efficiency-oriented approaches to judicial resolution of conflicting property rights. Posner writes of the modern approach to problems of constitutional enactment and interpretation in a passage reminiscent of the "constitutional economics" of Nobel Laureate James M. Buchanan.

> The Constitution is often discussed as a kind of contract and related to other non-standard contracts such as the "social contract." . . . The design and interpretation of constitutions, when viewed from an economic standpoint, involve a tension between efficiency and democracy.

Efficiency in Posner's view is maximized by a constitution that confines government to a least-cost approach of preventing the occurrence of negative events while simultaneously encouraging the occurrence of positive events. The spirit or scope of such a government, he says, is limited or narrowed by constitutions rather than democratically unfettered and broad. Advocates of limited government worry that a democracy without clearly defined limits tempts coalitions to take control of government and use it to expropriate the wealth of people who do not belong to those coalitions.

The Virginia Declaration seems to prefigure these concerns by raising two key issues: How does any group of constitutional framers insure that any later public understands that the constitution sets forth precepts that were intended to favor posterity as well as the framing generation? How does the generation of framers make any later public understand that no generation has the right to deprive subsequent generations of the constitutional protections that are the legacy of some prior framing generation's foresight? These questions matter because property and property rights raise issues of intergenerational equity.

Mason and the Virginians saw to it that future generations would be reminded that the enactments of the framing generation are entitled to greater respect and deference than those of subsequent generations. They made this point by the reference to "frequent recurrence to fundamental principles" in the 15th paragraph of the Virginia Declaration. Paragraph 15 also carries forward the main thrust of the spirit of all the English constitutional documents of the past. The assertion of fundamental constitutional rights amounts to an ongoing renewal of the demand that the king or other rulers observe the ancient and customary laws. Those laws are the natural rights and liberties of free Englishmen, as modified by the common law, which prevailed before the Norman Conquest in 1066.

The most progressive feature of the Virginia Declaration stands in contrast to this reference to ancient rights. Rather, the provision guaranteeing the free exercise of religion in paragraph 16 carries forward points the Levellers raised in England nearly 150 years earlier in the Agreement of the People, but in an even more liberal manner.

THE DECLARATION OF INDEPENDENCE

In May 1776, the delegates to the Virginia state constitutional convention in Williamsburg approved a resolution in favor of independence. One of the Virginia delegates to the Continental Congress in Philadelphia, Richard Henry Lee, introduced the Virginia resolution June 7, 1776. John Adams seconded it.

Debate began the next day and continued through June 10, when a committee, which included John Adams, Benjamin Franklin, and Thomas Jefferson, was appointed to draft a declaration.

Meanwhile, the debate was adjourned until July 1 to allow delegates from the middle states that were not yet committed to independence, such as New York and New Jersey, to receive new instructions. (In Virginia and New England, there was no doubt).

At the request of the committee, Jefferson drafted the Declaration. When he sat down to write, he would have had access to copies of the final version of the Virginia Constitution and George Mason's Declaration of Rights. They had been adopted June 12, 1776, and reprinted in the Philadelphia *Pennsylvania Evening Post*. He also had available copies of his own draft constitution for Virginia. (Portions of Jefferson's draft survived in the final version of the Virginia Constitution, especially Chapter II, section I, which is analogous to the indictment of King George III in his draft of the Declaration of Independence.)

The Declaration of Independence has four distinct parts. First, there is the preamble, the portion most often memorized and quoted. It is a compendium of John Locke's phraseology about natural law as Trenchard and Gordon understood it. Second, there is the indictment of King George III, which makes up about 60 percent of the document. This is a litany of complaints about British administration of the North American colonies, blaming the king individually for those matters.

Third, there is a recapitulation, which states a brief history of American petitions to Parliament and the king and of their rejection. Finally, there is the declaration, in which the colonies declare their independence. The recapitulation and declaration, taken together, are about as long as the famous preamble.

Property and property rights are mentioned nowhere in the preamble. They figure prominently in the indictment clauses, referring to the king's retention of the power to give final approval to local laws, the refusal of immigration measures that would encourage more settlement in America, and the imposition of taxes on the colonists without their consent.

It is arguable that property rights also are intended to be included within the general phrase, "the pursuit of happiness," a concept that was listed separately from the right of property in Mason's Virginia Declaration. All the Continental Congress delegates except John Dickinson signed the Declaration, and many of them had substantial property interests. Almost certainly, they would not have signed it if they believed that they were signing away any or all of their claims to the protection and enjoyment of property. John Adams, no enemy of property, was the foremost advocate of Jefferson's draft on the floor of the Congress.

Jefferson, however, did not explicitly mention property rights. The fullest published explanation of Jefferson's choice of words on this point comes from historian Dumas Malone, writing about Jefferson's reaction to another milestone document, Lafayette's draft of the French Declaration of the Rights of Man (1789).

According to Malone's *Jefferson and the Rights of Man* (Little Brown, 1951) Jefferson's reasons for wanting to omit the word property from the 1789 French document, Malone says, were the same as his reasons for using the expression "pursuit of happiness" in the Declaration of Independence. He was not disposed to attack property as an institution, quite to the contrary. In pre-revolutionary Paris, Malone says, Jefferson reported several times that the sanctity of property was generally respected by the populace. Malone continues: "But he still regarded property, like government, as a means to human happiness—not as an end in itself, not a natural and inalienable right in the same sense as the life and liberty of a person. He wanted to keep first things first."

The principal deletions that the Continental Congress made in Jefferson's draft concerned his condemnations of the slave trade. Before Independence, several colonies had attempted to outlaw the international slave trade by legislation, but the king had failed to approve the laws. Under the Constitution and at the time of Independence, slaves were chattel property.

In the Congress, South Carolina and other southern colonies made it plain that they would not agree to the Declaration unless Jefferson's offending draft clauses on slavery were removed. Those colonies deemed the international slave trade essential to their continued economic well-being. Recalling the Congress in 1821, Jefferson wrote that some northern delegates, too, were "a little tender" on the subject, "for though their people had very few slaves themselves yet they had been pretty considerable carriers of them to others."

Jefferson asserted that Northern delegates preferred to strike his antislavery clauses because of the profitable Northern trade in carrying slaves in ships both to North America and from the Northern to the Southern colonies.

Another clause from the original draft that was changed on the floor of

Congress comprised Jefferson's complaints against the moral blindness and deafness of the British people. Jefferson's original was more strongly worded than the final version that Congress approved.

In sum, the Declaration of Independence does not explicitly protect property rights. But modern American property rights—in the sense of what remains of the classical liberal conception of property rights—probably would have been impossible without the Declaration.

JOHN ADAMS AND THE MASSACHUSETTS CONSTITUTION

John Adams (1735-1826), one of the men who helped draft the Declaration, became a delegate to the Massachusetts constitutional convention in September 1779. He eventually became the sole draftsman of the state's constitution. Copies of his draft were printed and distributed to the convention October 30, 1779.

A devotee of the principles of liberty derived from the English civil wars of the 17th century, Adams deliberately decided to call Massachusetts a *commonwealth*, not a *state*. The legal distinction was of no great practical difference but was intended to recall the form of English government of Cromwell's time. No one seriously questioned the name Adams selected.

Adams already had been abroad as a member of the American ministerial delegation in Paris, and he drew on this fund of knowledge and personal experience in drafting the Massachusetts Constitution of 1780. It is a compendium of distilled wisdom. In most instances, Adams restated points made earlier by the Virginians even better than they did or addressed points that they did not address explicitly.

The principal and glaring exception is how Adams dealt with religion and, in Massachusetts, the non-separation of church and state.

At the time, there were two influential views regarding religion and the state. The New England view, reflected in Adams's draft of the Massachusetts Constitution, reflected the strong legal standing given to religious traditions by the Puritan fathers and the English Declaration of Right. The New England view tolerates a great deal of state interference in religious matters and makes religion the underpinning of morality within the state.

In contrast, the Virginia view prohibits the state from religious interference and assumes that moral beliefs are a matter of individual conscience beyond the power of the state to regulate.

It is sometimes assumed that the religious clauses of the First Amendment of the U.S. Constitution, as applied to the entire United States, are derived exclusively from a single unified view toward religion and the state. But this assumption is a mistake. Both the New England approach and the Virginia approach had proponents. Strictly speaking, all that the relevant part of the First Amendment of the U.S. Constitution prohibited was a *federal* establishment of religion, or a *federal* prohibition of the free exercise of religion. The states still were left free to maintain established (i.e., state-supported) churches or to regulate (or, presumably, even to prohibit) the free or public exercise of religion.

History is open to interpretation about whether it was the New England or the Virginia approach that actually informed the framing of the First Amendment. All those who prefer to be left alone in the quiet enjoyment of their property and their liberties probably should endorse the traditional Virginia view (strict separation of church and state), while those more concerned with the promotion of community-oriented values probably should endorse the traditional New England view.

In classical liberal, Lockean theory, the rights of property are conferred by a man's labor, not by his religious preferences. The Virginia model of religious liberty as framed by Mason, and later elaborated by Jefferson and Madison, carries forward that classical liberal view. The New England view, expressed by Adams, at least opens the door to state taxes to support particular churches or denominations, to test oaths for voting or holding public office, and to religious regulation of land ownership.

The preamble that Adams drafted for the Massachusetts Constitution does not mention property expressly. Adams wrote that the purpose of government is to secure the existence of the *body politic* (reasonably understood to mean both the capacity for and the form of self-government) and to provide the members of that body "with the power of enjoying, in safety and tranquility, their natural rights, and the blessings of life. . . ." He treated "safety, prosperity, and happiness" as fundamental measures of governmental effectiveness.

Following the preamble, Adams gave a basic statement of fundamental rights and liberties that clearly ranks property rights as fundamental.

> All men are born free and equal, and have certain natural, essential and unalienable rights; among which may be reckoned the right of enjoying and defending their lives and liberties; that of acquiring, possessing, and protecting property; in fine, that of seeking and obtaining their safety and happiness.

In Virginia four years earlier, Mason used the phrase "the pursuit of happiness and safety." One surmises that, because Adams listed safety ahead of happiness, he assumed that one has to be safe before one can be happy.

Adams provided a greater exposition of governmental protection of property rights than Mason. His text specifies that each individual has a right to the protection of society in the enjoyment of his life, liberty, and property, "according to standing laws." In exchange for this protection, an individual must contribute "his share" of taxes to the public expenses and of "personal service . . . when necessary." Then Adams had a great insight:

> But no part of the property of an individual can, with justice, be taken from him, or applied to publick uses, without his own consent, or that of the representative body of the people. . . . And whenever the publick exigencies require, that the property of any individual should be appropriated to publick uses, *he shall receive a reasonable compensation therefor*. (Italics added.)

This is the conceptual breakthrough in the Anglo-American tradition for adequate protection of private property from governmental takings. This requirement was what had been missing all along as a deterrent to overreaching takings by the state. There are no uncompensated governmental takings of private property in John Adams's Massachusetts Constitution. This provision, more than Mason's version of a takings clause (requiring the property owner's consent only), is closest in spirit to the taking clause of the Fifth Amendment of the U.S. Constitution, which provides that private property shall not be taken for public use without just compensation.

It is a never-ending quest for any free people living under a constitutional form of government to balance the tension between necessary governmental processes and individual liberty. At the heart of the tension are the concepts of ordered liberty and the pursuit of happiness up to the limits of another person's rights. This requires a certain amount of government to assure safety and create an environment in which individual freedom can exist. To that end, Part I, Article XVIII of the Massachusetts Constitution rephrases Mason's list of the positive values that are hallmarks of free government.

> A frequent recurrence to the fundamental principles of the constitution, and a constant adherence to those of piety, justice, moderation, temperance, industry, and frugality are absolutely necessary to preserve the advantages of liberty, and

to maintain a free government.

Adams substituted "piety" for Mason's use of the word "virtue" and adds industry to the litany. In any case, the values listed are the traditional New England virtues and are appropriate for a New England constitution of the late 18th century. But Adams's list of civic virtues is just as essential today to liberty and good government as it was 230 years ago.

Going beyond Mason, Adams concluded the list of necessary civic virtues by enjoining his fellow citizens to "have a particular attention to all those principles" in selecting their public officials and to hold those officials to account for their conduct of office in "an exact and constant observance of them." This is sound advice for all generations.

THE NORTHWEST ORDINANCE

Following victory in the Revolution and the establishment of the independent United States, the new country continued to grow. New states were formed out of old and new territories. The first new state was Vermont (1791), carved from territory previously disputed between New Hampshire and New York.

The first state lying beyond the great forest of the Appalachians was Kentucky. Originally part of Virginia, it was first settled by Virginia and North Carolina men after 1767 and was admitted into the Union in 1792.

The next new state was Tennessee, originally part of North Carolina, first settled in 1769 and admitted into the Union in 1796.

In the Old Northwest, Ohio entered the Union in 1803. The first permanent white European settlement in Ohio was at Marietta, in 1788, promoted by the Ohio Company of Associates, a land company organized in Boston in 1786. Initially, New York, Massachusetts, Connecticut, and Virginia all claimed land in Ohio. The effort to resolve these claims, and also to enable the Ohio Company to begin to sell its land rights, helped lead Congress to pass legislation addressing the issues of settling new lands and creating states from them. Ohio became the first new state originally governed by the principal legislation, the Northwest Ordinance of 1787.

The Ordinance was another milestone document in American history and the history of property rights. It spelled out how future states would be created from the western lands and how they would enter the Union. It made clear that the rights won by the original 13 colonies in the Revolution would be extended to the citizens of the new states. By providing a legislative roadmap to convert territories into states and settlers into citizens, the Ordinance helped accelerate the westward expansion of the United States.

Thomas Jefferson, with the collaboration of James Madison, had drafted a primitive ordinance for the Northwest Territory in 1784. Several of his provisions survived in the final document. However, the final Ordinance is much more detailed. The most salient feature of Jefferson's draft that made its way into the final legislation is a prohibition of slavery in the Northwest Territory.

The final version of the Northwest Ordinance of 1787 was written by delegate Nathan Dane of Massachusetts, in consultation with the driving actor behind the Ohio Company of Associates, Dr. Manasseh Cutler of Hamilton, Massachusetts. The Ordinance aptly has been described as the last colonial charter, albeit one drafted in the American Congress itself. In greater detail than any other Anglo-American constitutional document since Magna Carta, the Northwest Ordinance deals explicitly with real and personal property rights. In fact, property rights issues dominate the document, with some progressive features not yet present in the constitutions of the original 13 states.

The document sets forth, in a manner reminiscent of Magna Carta, the inheritance rights to be observed in the Territory. All estates lying within the region were to be distributed in equal parts by lineal and natural descent, with equal representation for grandchildren of deceased parents and for all children of the deceased, including illegitimate children when parentage could be proven or presumed. There was to be no rule of primogeniture, such as prevailed in England and in some of the Colonies. Half-siblings were to be recognized as fully as siblings "of the whole blood." The intent of these provisions was to insure that large estates of land would not be held, or would be held only with difficulty, in one family for generation after generation, descending from eldest son to eldest son.

Women were assured equal inheritance rights with men, at least in intestate succession (estates without wills). The dower rights of women specified in Magna Carta also were preserved explicitly. Widows were to receive one-third life estates in real property and an absolute distribution of one-third of all personal property.

In other property matters, real estate conveyances had to be in writing and "signed, sealed, and delivered" by the holders of the estates, who themselves had to be legally competent adults. The conveyances had to be attested by two witnesses. These provisions of the Ordinance reiterated practices regarding written conveyances of real estate first put in place more than 100 years earlier in England with the Statute of Frauds (1677), under which delivery of a deed constituted the formal legal conveyance of real property.

Personal property was to be transferred legally by physical delivery. Wills and real estate conveyances were to be "proved and recorded" within one year after appropriate recording offices were established. Much of Kentucky and Tennessee had been settled without such recording offices, which generated many disputes about real property ownership and transfers. The Ordinance aimed to avoid similar controversies in the Northwest.

The Northwest Ordinance also provided for Congress to appoint a governor of the Northwest Territory and authorized the governor "to lay out [i.e., to survey] the parts of the district in which the Indian titles shall have been extinguished, into Counties and townships. . . ." It also called for the creation of a territorial legislature that could alter and regulate the governor's actions.

The Ordinance spells out what are essentially the basic laws that would apply in the Territory. Referring to these provisions, the Ordinance also says, "It is hereby Ordained and declared by the authority aforesaid, That the following articles shall be considered as Articles of compact between the original States and the people and states in the said territory, and forever remain unalterable, unless by common consent, to wit." A fair argument can be made (and, indeed, often is made in the courts of the Old Northwest states) that, unless the constitution of a state addresses a specific point of law, then the Northwest Ordinance is controlling on that point of law. The provision clarified the governing law affecting property in the absence of any new provision in state law.

The Ordinance includes the equivalent of a bill of rights for the Territory, one that abounds in property rights protections and resembles the list of fundamental rights that John Adams included in the Massachusetts Constitution. The taking clause (the provision affecting governmental acquisitions for public use) is written more broadly than the clause later included in the U.S. Constitution. The taking clause of the Fifth Amendment speaks explicitly only of property, but the taking clause of the Northwest Ordinance covers compulsory services, also. The conditions by which the government could take property by eminent domain were more restrictive under the Ordinance than commonly apply today. The Ordinance required "public exigencies [that] make it Necessary for the common preservation" before eminent domain could be invoked.

Today, in contrast, in the *Kelo v. New London* case (2005), the U.S. Supreme

Court laid down a much lower standard, upholding a Connecticut state law authorizing a taking (in that case for private use) when the objective was simply the development of commercial property in a residential or mixed use neighborhood.

The Ordinance's prohibition of slavery within the Territory still allowed fugitive slaves to be lawfully reclaimed—essentially a political sop to the southern states. Nevertheless, the Ordinance was a significant step forward on this point. At the time, both slavery and the slave trade were permitted in every existing state. The Northwest Ordinance provided for the creation of up to five states. By specifically prohibiting slavery, the Ordinance thereby guaranteed that eventually there would be five new states that excluded it.

6

The U.S. Constitution

Every state but Rhode Island sent delegates to the Constitutional Convention in Philadelphia in May 1787. Their mandate was to strengthen the Articles of Confederation, the first constitution of the United States. The Articles, which were drafted in 1777 and ratified by the states in 1781, left most of the powers of government with the states and gave the national government little authority. Although this arrangement could claim a few successes, such as the Northwest Ordinance, generally it did not work well because of the government's dependence on remittances from the states for funding. In addition, amendment of the Articles of Confederation required *unanimity* of the state legislatures, a high hurdle.

The goal of the Constitutional Convention was limited. It was supposed to provide for a more unified executive and to address potential civil disturbances similar to Shays' Rebellion. That rebellion arose in 1786 among farmers in western Massachusetts who objected to new taxes and farm mortgage foreclosures linked to payments of state bonds. Around 5,000 men engaged in militia training with the rebels, and they eventually launched a failed attack on the Springfield armory. The last skirmish of the rebellion occurred in Sheffield, Massachusetts, in early 1787, a few months before the Constitutional Convention convened.

The Convention also was charged with devising a more certain revenue stream for the national government than that provided by reliance on funding requisitions to the states.

The delegates almost immediately cast off the limits of their mandate and commenced a revision of the Articles tantamount to repeal. As a consequence, they created a document that provides a much stronger structure for military organization under congressional control, to be commanded by the chief executive. The military, in turn, was charged with defending the Constitution, which itself was seen as a bulwark for property rights, including rights to financial assets such as government bonds. When the delegates finally assembled at the appointed time, May 14, 1787, delegates from only a few states appeared, and a quorum was not reached until May 25, when delegates appeared from seven states.

One of the things they did in the new Constitution was to make it easier to change. The new document required that only *nine* of the 13 states ratify before the Constitution became effective. In order to circumvent the hostile legislatures of some states, the same article provided that separately elected *conventions* meet in each state for the purpose of considering ratification. Future amendments would require the ratification of three-fourths of the states. This promoted property rights by making changes in the fundamental bargain difficult, but not impossible, to obtain. This assured the stability of the structure protecting property interests.

The American Constitution was signed and adopted by the delegates on September 17, and ratified by the states in 1788. Just a few years later, in 1791, it was modified with the addition of the first 10 amendments—the Bill of Rights. All told it has been amended 27 times, most recently in 1992. That year, the second of the original 12 amendments first proposed in 1789 was ratified (the last ten were adopted as the Bill of Rights). The 27th Amendment prohibits a raise in congressional salaries from taking effect until after a new election (which occurs every two years) has intervened. The change gives the people a chance to vote against the senators and representatives who attempted to raise their own salaries.

Much of the original document and many of the amendments address fundamental issues of rights and liberty. A great deal of this content harks back to George Mason's 1776 list of classically liberal fundamental rights: life, liberty, property, safety, and the pursuit of happiness. The original Constitution addresses life, property, and safety issues; the Bill of Rights adds liberty and the pursuit of happiness. Throughout, property rights were a dominant theme in the Framers' minds.

With the possible exception of the roughly contemporaneous Northwest Ordinance, the Constitution and Bill of Rights elevated concern for the promotion and protection of property rights to an unprecedented degree. By providing an impartial federal forum for the resolution of disputes, together with the protection of contracts and the federal regulation of interstate and foreign commerce, the Constitution continues to give private property rights greater formal protection in the United States than in most other countries and, quite possibly, more than in any other country of the world.

The Constitution begins by invoking the authority or ultimate sovereignty of the people themselves, in whose name this Constitution is made ("We the People of the United States"). The objects or ends of the Constitution are specified as: "[T]o form a more perfect Union, establish Justice, insure domestic Tranquility, provide for the common defense, promote the general Welfare, and secure the Blessings of Liberty to ourselves and our Posterity."

Ordinarily preambles have no or little legal effect in construing the meaning of documents. But in this case, the Preamble contains one clause, the one referring to "the general Welfare," that together with a later clause risks rendering the rest of the Constitution meaningless. The other clause, at the end of Article I, section 8, gives to Congress the power "to make all Laws which shall be necessary and proper for carrying into Execution the foregoing Powers." Taken at face value, these two clauses would seem to confer on Congress the right to make any law deemed necessary and proper to promote the general welfare, no matter how tenuous the connection between the measure proposed and the explicitly enumerated powers of Congress.

Article I has 10 sections and generally covers all legislative powers. The article requires that both representation in the new Congress and all direct taxes Congress would impose on the people or their property be apportioned among the states by population. This preserved the principle of equality of rates of taxation. The article also insures that the people's direct representatives shall be accountable for all taxes by requiring that all revenue bills originate in the House.

Article I, section 8, requires close and careful study in connection with property rights because it is here that the Constitution states the *positive* powers of Congress. The section explicitly enumerates the economic powers of Congress as follows:

Taxation and defense powers.
Borrowing money on the credit of the United States.
Regulation of commerce.
Coining money, regulating its value and the value of foreign coin, and standardization of weights and measures.

Punishing the counterfeiting of U.S. securities and coin.

Establishing post offices and post roads (but notably *not* the power to cut canals or to charter corporations, powers that were considered and rejected at the Constitutional Convention).

Making patent and copyright laws.

Making all laws necessary and proper to carry into effect the foregoing powers.

Most of the rest of Article I, section 8, involves the defense—including the military defense—of life, liberty, property, and safety, as well as the resolution of disputes.

The list of congressional powers ends with the famed "necessary and proper" clause. This clause was the core of Jefferson's objections to Alexander Hamilton's (and later, John Marshall's) Federalist interpretation of the Constitution.

In simplified terms, Jefferson's view of implied powers in the Constitution was that only the most obvious and direct means, derived by logical and necessary implication, should be used in pursuit of governmental objectives. Hamilton (and Marshall as chief justice) argued that any means rationally designed to produce one of the enumerated constitutional ends were permitted to the federal government, as long as such means were not immoral, obviously illegal, and were somehow consistent with the overall spirit of the Constitution.

Since 1819 at the latest, the Supreme Court has tended to follow the Hamilton-Marshall interpretation. The impact of the Court's wide-ranging approach has been to empower wartime suspensions of habeas corpus (the Civil War), to endorse central economic planning during wartime (World War I) and in peacetime (the New Deal), and to pave the way for a large system of social welfare payments, all of which tend to undermine property rights.

Another key section in Article I lists exactly what Congress may *not* do. Among other things, Congress may not pass any *direct* tax except in proportion to the most recent census figures. No federal income tax—graduated or otherwise—was to be allowed. This was substantially changed in 1913, when the 16th Amendment gave Congress the right to ignore equal apportionment among states by population when taxing the American people. The original system of taxation required Congress either to rely on *indirect* taxes (on consumption and imports, for example) or to impose *direct* taxes (payable by each business or individual) only at an equal rate for all taxpayers regardless of income or wealth.

Article I also lists what the states may not do. The states shall not pass laws that target an individual or his property, impair contracts (potentially an important protection of property rights) or establish feudal estates or inherited offices. They also shall not conduct foreign affairs, engage in maritime war, or issue their own currency (the latter was done widely before the Constitution was adopted).

In addition, the states are banned from passing legal tender laws for anything except gold and silver coin; however, bullion is excepted and cannot be made legal tender. This means that state legislatures could proclaim bullion or anything else a form of money lawful for commerce, exchange, and the payment of taxes. But the states cannot *require* private persons to accept anything other than gold or silver coins. A legal tender law requiring the acceptance of alternative forms of money usually affects property rights negatively by requiring an exchange of things of value for things of lesser value.

The Constitution does not prohibit Congress from authorizing legal tender paper money. When this issue was debated in Philadelphia, even George Mason agreed that the hands of Congress should not be tied *in an emergency* on this point.

Article II governs executive power. The principal protection of property within Article II is that an electoral college, essentially controlled by the states, is interposed between the president and the people. This provision paves the way for property interests having greater influence on presidential elections than if the people voted directly for the president. Underpopulated states gain proportionately greater influence by having two senators counted in allocations of electoral votes among the states. The presumption is that both senators and presidential electors tend to be drawn from classes of people who favor property rights.

Article III addresses the judiciary. The key inclusion that affects property rights is the definition of the general jurisdiction of the federal courts, potentially conferring jurisdiction on the federal courts when a resident of one state is sued in the state courts of another state. Federal statutes usually fix a minimum amount in controversy (currently $75,000) before actions filed in state court may be moved to federal court. Out-of-state defendants usually prefer federal courts because of the presumptively higher quality of the judges in federal courts and because of the uniform national rules of procedure there.

Article IV is a catch-all statement of principles for the federal government's "general supervision" of interstate relations. It mandates that each state shall give full legal recognition to the official documents of any other state. This means that people do not have to prove legal title to recorded and movable property (for example, automobiles) when crossing state lines.

Article VI ratifies the debts of the Confederation as valid debts of the United States under the Constitution. This measure was intended to reassure holders of national debt instruments.

It also establishes the precedent, which came into play during the financial crisis that began in August 2007, that the full faith and credit of the federal government stands behind all of its obligations. In 2008, the provision was used to justify the government bailout and takeover of mortgage giants Fannie Mae and Freddie Mac. The enterprises were not part of the government, but officials said that helping them would safeguard the Treasury's own credit standing.

Originally, the provision meant that persons buying government debt under one Congress can have confidence that the debt will be honored under any subsequent Congress. Without this confidence, the Treasury would find it nearly impossible to sell its debt instruments in the open market.

The Constitution also opened the way for financing debt repayments within its taxation and monetary provisions, a marked improvement over requisitions to the states, the means used under the Confederation.

Article VI also makes the Constitution, laws, and treaties of the United States the supreme law of the land, and binds the judges of every state to observe federal supremacy over the constitutions and laws of their states. To the extent that property rights exist under federal law, property owners are assured of equal enforcement in every state.

THE BILL OF RIGHTS

One of the first actions of the new Congress, prompted by Representative James Madison of Virginia, was to approve and submit to the states a proposed Bill of Rights. Approximately 80 amendments were initially proposed by the states. They were whittled down to 17 in the House and then finally to 12 in conference with the Senate on September 25, 1789. After adoption by the Congress, they were sent out to the states. By December 15, 1791, 11 states, or one state more than the three-fourths required, had ratified 10 of the amendments. (The two that were rejected covered a formula for increasing the ratio of population to members of the House of Representatives and the timing of salary increases for members of Congress. Remarkably, the latter was finally ratified in 1992, 203 years after it was first proposed.)

The 10 amendments became known as the Bill of Rights. The content of eight of them is relevant to property rights. An explicit protection for property appears in the Fifth Amendment, and the protection is implicit in seven others. In several instances, an amendment makes no sense unless it is construed as intending a protection of property rights. At the federal level, most of the protections of property rights that the public enjoys rest on the Bill of Rights.

The idea that explicit protections of liberties, including property rights, needed to be codified in a federal Bill of Rights stirred controversy at the Constitutional Convention. A common argument, expressed by delegate James Wilson of Pennsylvania, was that the Constitution needed no Bill of Rights. The general spirit of liberalism of the Age of Enlightenment was thought to be a sufficient guarantee of the people's liberties and property.

Others argued that the enumeration of liberties in a Bill of Rights was dangerous because it could be construed as a lack of confidence in the protection afforded by the original Constitution.

James Madison set forth the main argument against a Bill of Rights in *The Federalist*, No. 10 (1787). He wrote that the various checks and balances provided in the Constitution should suffice to prevent unwarranted usurpations of power or infringements on liberty and property. Madison also noted that differences in the capacity to acquire and retain property gave rise to factions in the body politic. He suggested that, in a large republic such as the United States, only separations of power and checks and balances effectively could prevent encroachments by majority factions on the rights of minority factions. He identified redistributions of property and the issuance of paper money as "wicked schemes" that checks and balances should be able to prevent.

On the other side of the debate, a group at the Philadelphia convention led by Virginia's George Mason argued that the absence of an effective Bill of Rights in the original Constitution was sufficient reason for voting against it. Mason also wanted more separation of power between the executive and legislative branches and greater checks on the exercise of executive power.

Thomas Jefferson, then the U.S. minister to France and still in Paris, wrote to Madison and others that he shared Mason's doubts about the centralization of federal power provided for in the original Constitution. But he wrote that prompt adoption of necessary amendments would assuage his fears. The strategy that he suggested was that the two largest and most important states, Virginia and New York, should withhold their ratifications of the Constitution until it was clear that Congress would submit a Bill of Rights to the states. To address Mason's concerns about federal power versus the rights of the states directly, Jefferson endorsed what became the Ninth and Tenth Amendments, explicitly reserving unenumerated powers of the federal government to the states or to the people. In somewhat slipshod fashion, Jefferson's strategy was the one followed, the Constitution was ratified, and the Bill of Rights promptly was submitted to the states.

PROPERTY RIGHTS PROVISIONS IN THE BILL OF RIGHTS

The First Amendment of the Constitution is a basic statement of fundamental liberties that also protects property rights in a number of ways. The prohibition of a federal establishment of religion makes these rights safer because the prohibition ensures that there will be no church taxes or mandatory tithes. In addition, no one can be taxed because of the form of his religious worship, nor can federal taxes be laid on the exercise of free speech or on books and newspapers.

The people are allowed to assemble peaceably. Whether or not in assembly, they may petition their government without being charged with seditious libel or treason. Both provisions make it possible for people to discuss plans for the defense of their property and to present those plans to Congress and the executive branch.

The Second Amendment's assertion of the right to bear arms spoke directly to property rights at the time of the amendment's creation. The Framers, particularly men of the South and West such as Jefferson and Madison, understood the need of every frontier family to have firearms at home for the defense of life and property. They supported the idea of a citizen militia as well as the personal possession of firearms. The modern dispute about the Second Amendment centers on whether the people have a right to bear arms outside a militia context. But a 2008 Supreme Court decision (*District of Columbia v. Heller*) makes it reasonably clear that the right to bear arms is personal and does not depend on membership in a militia.

The Third Amendment protects private property by prohibiting the non-consensual quartering of soldiers in any house in peacetime or in war except according to law.

The Fourth Amendment's prohibition against unreasonable searches and seizures frames *privacy* as a *property rights* issue, as John Adams would have understood it. The amendment forbids general search warrants and sets rules for special warrants. These require sworn oaths by persons having actual knowledge of relevant facts, probable cause, and specific descriptions.

Unfortunately, the wonderful clause that Adams added to the Massachusetts Constitution, protecting the people's personal possessions as well, was omitted. The Fourth Amendment, as currently interpreted, basically allows the police to stop and search any automobile or schools to search students' lockers on almost any pretext. The legal rationale is that the expectation of *privacy* supposedly is lower in an automobile or for a school locker than in a home. But what about the *property right?*

The due process clause of the Fifth Amendment is the heart of modern property rights protection under the U.S. Constitution. The amendment restates ancient principles set forth in Magna Carta, that no person shall be deprived of fundamental rights (here enumerated as life, liberty, and property) without due process of law, at least at the federal level.

Unlike the Fourth Amendment, the taking clause of the Fifth Amendment does reflect the high level of protection of John Adams's Declaration of Rights in the Massachusetts Constitution. This requires both consent and "reasonable compensation" for any taking of private property for public use.

The Seventh Amendment guarantees the right of trial by jury in civil lawsuits where the amount in controversy is more than $20. Congress periodically raises that dollar amount, and the minimum value currently required is $75,000. (Cases involving parties from different states are addressed in Article III of the main body of the Constitution, which allows federal jurisdiction over controversies about property. The minimum amount required also is $75,000.)

The costs of jury trials are fairly large in comparison to the amounts in controversy, and the United States now is the only industrial nation that regularly uses juries in private cases.

Nevertheless, the right of trial by jury in civil cases was held to be *sacred* by both George Mason and John Adams in the Declarations of Rights drafted for their states. Mason even went so far as to specify the *ancient* trial by jury of 12 men. Classical liberals of the Framers' generation apparently saw the value of the protection of liberty and property rights as outweighing any calculus balancing the efficiency of the jury system versus the alternatives.

The Ninth Amendment reiterates the existence of fundamental rights for individuals that are not enumerated in the Constitution. At least, that was the traditional interpretation until the New Deal. In *United States v. Carolene*

Products Co. (1938), the Supreme Court stated that it would defer in matters of economic regulation to statutes having "some rational basis" unless the regulation contravened "a specific prohibition of the Constitution, such as those of the first ten Amendments." The Court will not invalidate economic regulations unless they specifically violate some enumerated provision of the Bill of Rights.

It has proven comparatively easy for economic regulators to write language that carefully steps around property rights protections. The current Supreme Court leans somewhat in the direction of a post-New Deal, almost post-modern theory that there are *no* fundamental rights or liberties *unless* they are specifically enumerated in the Constitution, or derived from the enumerated rights by necessary and unavoidable deduction. This is classical liberalism stood on its head. It shifts the burden of resisting obnoxious economic regulation to the individual property owner instead of requiring the government to justify its conduct.

The Tenth Amendment assigns all rights to the states and to the people that are neither specifically delegated nor prohibited to the federal government by the Constitution. As with the Ninth Amendment since the New Deal, federal courts have ruled consistently that the Tenth Amendment has no content.

The high water mark (or the morally low point) of federal regulation was reached in *Wickard v. Filburn* (1942), where an Ohio farmer was deemed to be engaged in *interstate commerce* (subject to federal regulation) by growing his own grain, keeping some for seed for the next year's crop, selling some locally, making his own flour, and feeding the rest to his own animals. The Court's reasoning was that such an independent farmer nevertheless influences the prices of agricultural products by withholding his own produce from the channels of interstate commerce, which the Constitution gives Congress the power to regulate.

Other Supreme Court decisions give the Executive pretty much a free rein in the conduct of foreign affairs, including trade (*United States v. Curtiss-Wright Export Corp.*, 1936).

But even before the New Deal, the last two amendments of the Bill of Rights were under siege. Since the early 19th century, various rulings of the Supreme Court have seemed to allow the federal government to do pretty much whatever it wants in the general domain of regulating commerce. In an 1819 ruling (*McCulloch v. Maryland*), the Supreme Court gave the federal government nearly a free hand in the exercise of powers not enumerated in the

Constitution or Bill of Rights. To paraphrase the government's own argument in *McCulloch*, having such broad powers in reserve gives the government the potential to destroy any person's property rights because, thanks to Supreme Court rulings, the intended checks and balances, such as the Ninth and Tenth Amendments, are ineffective barriers against federal encroachments on those rights.

A fair argument could be made that it would be better—less misleading to the public and more efficient for government administration, at least—to repeal the Ninth and Tenth Amendments, and perhaps even the guaranty clause of Article IV, which guarantees to every state a "republican form of government." However, one still might argue, and indeed one probably should, that it is an intellectual, a moral, and even a practical mistake *not* to enforce these provisions.

OTHER RELEVANT AMENDMENTS

Amendments made after the Bill of Rights also affect the property rights of Americans.

The 11th Amendment (1795) prohibits suits by the citizens of one state, or by foreign citizens, against any other state in any forum except the courts of the state being sued. This sometimes is referred to as the "state sovereign immunity" amendment.

The 13th Amendment (1865) is the first of three consecutive amendments that address slavery or the treatment of people as property. (The legal status of slaves from the time of the Founding Fathers through Reconstruction is summarized in the next section.) This amendment prohibits slavery and involuntary servitude (except as punishment for crimes) anywhere subject to the jurisdiction of the United States. Slavery was prohibited when the United States acquired the new territories of Alaska (1867), Hawaii (1898), the Philippines (1898), Puerto Rico (1898), Guam (1898), and other territories and island possessions.

The 14th Amendment (1868) modified a section of Article IV of the Constitution that addressed the "privileges and immunities" of citizenship. The thrust of the first section of the amendment is to guarantee equality before the law and equality of civil rights to all citizens of the United States, including equal protection of the law and due process of law. In essence, this was designed to secure the rights of former slaves and overturned *Dred Scott v. Sanford* (1857), which excluded slaves and their descendants from the rights of citizenship.

The exact terms of the guarantees apply to "persons." In 1886, the Supreme Court ruled "without discussion" (*Santa Clara County v. Southern Pacific Railroad*) that under the 14th Amendment *corporations* (fictive legal persons) were "persons" entitled to the same legal protections as living individual persons and citizens. Proofreader double checked your facts.

From that tiny acorn, the mature oak tree of full legal protection (and, some would argue, judicial *favoritism*) for modern American business corporations has grown. It is worth remembering that early corporations did not have perpetual charters. Nor did they have limited liability of shareholders, officers, and directors. Shares had substantial par value, and shareholders of financial corporations could be assessed for double the par value of their stock if their corporations failed. Early corporations also lacked the benefit of the modern "business judgment" rule, which exempts officers and directors from personal liability for good-faith decisions made in the ordinary course of business, with due care, and in the general interests of their corporations. In fact, until the second half of the 20th century, most businesses were *not* organized as corporations; they were organized as sole proprietorships, partnerships, or voluntary associations instead.

Yet judicial favoritism for business corporations was a hallmark of politics throughout the 19th century. It was supported by Federalists (Hamilton and Marshall), Whigs (Henry Clay and Daniel Webster), and Republicans (Abraham Lincoln, Roscoe Conkling, and Mark Hanna). Perhaps this favoritism was understandable in the interests of promoting greater economic efficiency. However, some legal scholars argue that such judicial favoritism makes little or no economic, moral, or legal sense for corporations that threaten to become monopolies and thereby, in this view, less than optimally efficient.

The 14th Amendment also deals with readmission of the rebel states (the Southern Confederacy) to the Union, which required repudiation of the Southern states' debts. The property rights of Southern creditors were affected, but the winners got to make the rules.

The 15th Amendment (1870) gave the right to vote in both federal and state elections to both freedmen whose freedom preceded the Civil War and to the recently freed slaves. It states that the right to vote shall not be denied on account of "race, color, or previous condition of servitude." But it did *not* extend this right to women, and Susan B. Anthony was arrested for attempting to vote in the New York congressional election in 1872 under the purported authority of the 15th Amendment.

The right to vote is an important protection of property rights for any class of persons, especially those previously disenfranchised, because those persons can vote for candidates who would reverse previously discriminatory patterns of conduct. The popular vote is a significant part of the checks and balances that make government function in accordance with the popular will. Within 100 years, the Constitution would have two additional amendments that addressed voter enfranchisement.

The 19th Amendment (1919) gave women the right to vote in both federal and state elections. This amendment effectively reversed the Susan B. Anthony case.

The 24th Amendment (1964) prohibited the states from enforcing poll taxes or any other taxes as a condition of voting in federal general or primary elections. At the time of the amendment's passage some Southern states still had poll or head taxes, intended to dissuade blacks (and poor whites) from voting.

A final amendment that has had a powerful effect on property rights is the 16th (1913), which gave Congress the power to levy an income tax. Specifically, it authorizes Congress to ignore apportionment among the states according to the Census when laying direct taxes on the American people. This language authorized a federal income tax (regardless of whether flat or progressive) for the first time other than during the emergency measures of the Civil War. Originally, the highest rate was 7 percent; currently, the highest rate is 35 percent, but it was as high as 94 percent during World War II and 91 percent for 1963.

SLAVERY AND PROPERTY RIGHTS, MARCH 5, 1770, TO APRIL 11, 1877

The Boston Massacre, March 5, 1770, counted among its victims one Crispus Attucks, a black man said to be of mixed African and Native American Indian heritage. Reputed to be a runaway slave working on a merchant sailing vessel, he was recorded as a sailor at the time of his death. The first black man to die in the cause of American freedom, his name was known to the Founding Fathers and Framers of the Constitution.

In the complaint portion of the Declaration of Independence, Thomas Jefferson's original draft contained language that he later described thus, writing in 1821:

The clause, too, reprobating the enslaving the inhabitants of Africa, was struck out in complaisance to South Carolina and Georgia, who had never attempted to restrain the importation of slaves, and who, on the contrary, still wished to continue it. Our Northern brethren also, I believe, felt a little tender under those censures; for though their people had very few slaves themselves, yet they had been pretty considerable carriers of them to others.

No writing better sums up the conflicted interests, beliefs, and objectives of the founding generation regarding the institution of chattel slavery, by that time focused nearly entirely on persons of African descent.

Slaves had been imported into the future United States since 1619 at the Jamestown, Virginia, colony. In the 1660s in the West Indies and following King Philip's War in North America in 1676, slave codes were adopted that imposed the condition of slavery through descent from a slave mother. Standards varied from state to state, but generally one-eighth African blood sufficed to hold one in an enslaved condition. After Independence, slavery gradually diminished in the North, and the legal importation of new slaves was prohibited after 1808. Illegal importations continued, however, usually by way of Cuba, until the Emancipation Proclamation became effective January 1, 1863.

The racial prejudices of the age determined the racial views of the founding generation. But it is fair to characterize the attitudes of Founding Fathers from North Carolina northward as following what they deemed an enlightened moderation. They believed that the institution of slavery would die off over time if new importations could be prohibited, which actually happened while Jefferson still was president in 1808. Jefferson, Madison, and others favoring western expansion of the United States saw to it that slavery would be prohibited in the Northwest Territory, which ultimately became the six states of Indiana, Illinois, Michigan, Minnesota, Ohio, and Wisconsin.

Mixed-race couples were allowed to live in Kentucky and Tennessee and in the Northwest, but not generally in the Eastern states below the Mason-Dixon line (Pennsylvania-Maryland border).

On the other hand, die-hard defenders of the institution of slavery made sure that the Old Southwest—Alabama, Florida, Kentucky, Mississippi, and Tennessee—allowed slavery. The admission of new states created from the Louisiana Purchase and from Texas created tensions about the expansion of slavery leading to the Civil War. During that era, enlightened moderates, both North and South, including Chief Justice John Marshall of Virginia, Senator Henry Clay of Kentucky, and attorney and sometime legislator Abraham

Lincoln from Illinois, tended to favor emigration of freed slaves. Various schemes included Back to Africa (the creation of colonies in Liberia and Sierra Leone), settlement in Central America, and settlement in the Indian territory of the High Plains.

During the early phases of the Civil War, Northern moderates encouraged President Lincoln to make an offer to purchase the Southern slaves in order to reduce or avoid bloodshed. There were about 4 million slaves at the time—including those in the border states that did not secede such as Kentucky and Missouri—within a total national population of about 31 million. It is far from clear that the hotheads in South Carolina would have accepted such an offer anyway. Lincoln finally got around to making an offer called "compensated emancipation" for the Border States, to be combined with a scheme involving the colonization by blacks of Panama, in March-April 1862. But by that time, too much blood had been shed on both sides for cool deliberation on the matter. Abolitionists considered the proposal a scheme to perpetuate slavery and a sellout of the blood already spilled. A bill offering compensated emancipation only within the District of Columbia became law April 16, 1862.

Five months later, the Emancipation Proclamation freed slaves without compensation in Southern states under military occupation. The Proclamation, which was issued on September 22, followed the Union army's victory of sorts at Antietam, Maryland, a few days earlier. In February 1865, two months before the war ended and Lincoln was assassinated, Congress finally submitted the 13th Amendment—which prohibited slavery without compensation—to the states. The amendment was ratified December 18.

During Reconstruction, which lasted until Union army forces were withdrawn and the Democratic Party assumed control of the state government in the last Southern state—South Carolina on April 11, 1877—former slaves were freed in place and were not required to emigrate. In the rebellious states, race-centered conflicts over voting, running for public office, public education, property ownership, taxation of real property, and eligibility for employment in certain lines of business and professions persisted as late 1977 and the inauguration of President Jimmy Carter of Georgia. Carter was the first president to bring large numbers of obviously well-qualified black citizens into national office since the end of Reconstruction.

Freedmen voted, held public office, and could defend their property more or less effectively during Reconstruction. But it was not until the third quarter of the 20th century that they and their descendants effectively exercised those rights again throughout most of the Old South. By then, a large number of the formerly black-owned farms in that region had been sold or lost.

REFLECTIONS ON THE CONSTITUTION

The U.S. Constitution is not a perfect document, particularly from the perspective of the protection of property rights. But it goes quite far in the direction of such protection, as originally drafted, as originally intended, and as originally understood. It embodies the classical liberal virtues of "justice, moderation, temperance, frugality, and [civic] virtue," using George Mason's phraseology about what is desirable in constitutional documents.

The Constitution is *not* a blueprint explicitly authorizing many aspects of contemporary life. Among these: central economic planning, progressive income taxation, military conscription for service abroad, the federal promotion and nourishment of corporations, or even that bane of 20th century property rights, land-use zoning.

The men who drafted the Constitution were as representative a body of the intellectual capacities of the leading men of the nation as it would have been possible to assemble. They made nearly all the right arguments from classical liberal perspectives on both (or several) sides of each major question. And they usually preserved a reasonable, coherent, internally consistent view of fundamental rights—namely, the right to life, liberty, property, safety, and the pursuit of happiness, using Mason's phraseology again.

After 1788, many of the founding generation such as George Mason, Patrick Henry, and Governor George Clinton of New York fell into the anti-Federalist camp. They were reasonably alarmed by what they viewed as the centralization of power in the proposed federal government. Proponents of the Constitution and a strong central government such as James Madison and Alexander Hamilton, working with the blessing and intense interest of George Washington himself, set about to reassure the public that enough divisions of power were included to enable nearly all previously existing liberties to be preserved. For further reassurance these same men made sure to adopt the Bill of Rights.

Some initial skeptics, such as Jefferson, eventually came around to the view that it was not the Constitution that was imperfect. (By 1790, he believed that it was quite a good document). Rather, the problem was the influence of men such as Hamilton and, later, Chief Justice John Marshall in *interpreting* and *applying* the Constitution.

From the perspective of those who support classical liberalism, Jefferson's view of the Constitution was correct. But Hamilton and Marshall were also true patriots whose views were understandable in the circumstances of their times. However, Hamilton crossed a Rubicon of constitutional interpretation in 1791, when he proposed to create a national bank to provide the government with a reliable source of credit. It was not clear whether Congress had the authority to charter such a bank. Such authority was not explicitly mentioned in the Constitution. But Hamilton argued that the government could exercise "implied powers," or powers that were not explicitly granted, as long as the powers were used to take "necessary and proper" actions to promote the "general welfare" (phrases taken from the Preamble and the end of Article I, Section 8). Hamilton and his followers, perhaps unwittingly, set in motion a train of events that fostered big government and favored big businesses.

Among other things, the turmoil of the French Revolution and the fierce arguments the Revolution made for the redistribution of private property strengthened the assaults on classical liberalism begun by the Federalists. Only Jeffersonian strict constructionist arguments would have provided a safe constitutional bulwark against the onslaughts of the 19th century.

Once one has embarked on the path of progressivism in constitutional interpretation, how does one know when one has taken a step too far? The only safe course is not to take the first step. Jefferson hammered home this point in a then-secret letter he wrote on February 15, 1791, to George Washington, in which he expressed his opposition to Hamilton's national bank plan. Restating an argument made earlier by Madison, Jefferson wrote:

> I consider the foundation of the Constitution as laid on this ground: That "all powers not delegated to the United States, by the Constitution, nor prohibited by it to the States, are reserved to the States or to the people." [This is a quotation from what later that year became the 10th Amendment.] To take a single step beyond the boundaries thus specially drawn around the powers of Congress, is to take possession of a boundless field of power, no longer susceptible of any definition.

For proponents of property rights, Jefferson's words outline the crux of the constitutional interpretation issue.

There are those who advocate the view of the Constitution as a living, evolving thing, constantly reshaping itself to meet the demands of each new generation. But they should bear the burden of informing each new generation of *exactly how far is too far* before they begin their journey of constitutional transformation. That is what Mason and Adams meant by "frequent recurrence to fundamental principles." Instead, such advocates tend to leave it to the general public to guess where the limits are. Meanwhile, they increasingly render the public defenseless against government promotion of big business and big labor on the one side, and the excesses of redistributionists and disrespecters of property rights, on the other side.

7

The Long Decline: Property Rights, the Individual, and the State

The adoption of the U.S. Constitution and the almost immediate recommendation of a Bill of Rights for ratification by the states struck some parts of Europe like a thunderbolt. In France and the British Isles, the political and philosophical outlook was analogous to dry kindling wood awaiting the spark from America. The philosophical and legal structures of property rights were a proportionately greater issue in America because there was vastly more property to allocate to newcomers than anywhere in Europe. It was natural for the early documents of the American founding to deal extensively with property rights.

In Europe, the philosophical basis for a rethinking of property rights had to be laid before any political or legal structures for reallocation could be constructed. The Scottish Enlightenment, the elaboration of Whig party thought in England during the 18th century, and the parliamentary debates in London during the American Revolution brought these issues to the fore in the British Isles.

In France, the debate on property rights more or less followed the British lead until the 1780s. The philosophical "wind from America" raised the prospect of an actual rebellion against the established order of things once French public finances deteriorated at the end of the Old Regime. By 1789, the philosophical spark caused the kindling to burst into flame. Nothing has been the same in the Old World or, for that matter, in the philosophical world of property rights, ever since.

Because of the interruption of the peaceful evolution of ideas about property rights by the French Revolution, the drafting of the U.S. Constitution and the Bill of Rights constitutes the high water mark in the evolution of classical liberal notions of property rights. Even in America, new challenges to that evolution arose from the proto-utilitarian ideas of Alexander Hamilton. Following Hobbes, he essentially argued that a strong central government was necessary to guarantee and defend property. Following Jean-Jacques Rousseau and Jeremy Bentham, he also argued that a broad and barely constrained interpretation of the Constitution was necessary to give that government all the powers that such a guarantee and such a defense would require.

Responding to Hamilton's formal assault on classical liberal ideas of limited government, Thomas Jefferson and James Madison organized the ancestral form of modern American political parties. At the time, roughly 1791-1792, everyone involved agreed that the rise of political parties (called factions then) organized around competing regional or economic interests risked becoming the death knell for the republican experiment in ordered liberty.

Back in France, the Revolution, which initially proclaimed its devotion to the promotion of property rights for the common man, descended into the Reign of Terror, replete with unlimited issuance of inconvertible paper money and price controls enforced by the strictest penalties. In those circumstances, property rights became entirely dependent on the whims of those who controlled the apparatus of the state's military, police, intelligence, and terror operations.

The dominant reaction in England and America was to point to France as an illustration of what could happen anytime that attempts were made to redistribute existing property rights. For more than a generation, those who controlled British and European society saw to it that no threat to existing property rights could arise. In America, however, especially after the presidential election of 1800 in which Jefferson prevailed over John Adams, the tendency was continued toward liberalization of property rights. The common people enjoyed an increasingly greater share as the American frontier moved west, even as Hamilton's followers increasingly controlled the machinery of the American government and its financial structures.

THE FRENCH REVOLUTION, 1789-1795, AND THE FRENCH DECLARATION OF THE RIGHTS OF MAN AND THE CITIZEN (1791)

Thomas Jefferson was living in Paris when the French Revolution erupted in July 1789, as was the Marquis de Lafayette, the French soldier and statesman. Lafayette had served as one of Washington's generals and had met Jefferson in Virginia during the Revolutionary War. In January 1789, soon after the U.S. Constitution was ratified, the two men began to exchange thoughts on a

French declaration of rights.

Other French noblemen, chief among them the scientist and mathematician the Marquis de Condorcet (1743-1794), also began working on a declaration, without being certain how they would use it or arrange to have it introduced into the turmoil of French politics just before the Revolution. Jefferson, who was recognized as an expert in such matters, eventually met with a number of parties interested in drafting a declaration or a constitution.

The first declaration to be approved by the National Assembly of France, in August 1789, was basically Lafayette's draft. It was influenced by his experience in America and his knowledge of George Mason's Virginia Declaration of Rights. After much debate and many political events, Condorcet, by then the secretary of the Assembly, steered a similar version through to approval in September 1791. This Declaration of the Rights of Man and the Citizen was added to the first French constitution by official publication of the two documents together September 14, 1791.

The Preamble to the Declaration (Condorcet's version) outlines "the natural and imprescriptible rights of man" as "liberty, property, safety, and resistance to oppression."

Unlike Mason's Virginia Declaration of Rights and the Declaration of Independence, the French document omits life and the pursuit of happiness. This omission should have been troubling to classical liberals of the late 18th century. Life might have been assumed to be a fundamental right of man, but it probably would have been best to say so explicitly. Still, persons familiar with the writings of John Locke could argue that a right to life presumptively was included within the right to resist oppression.

The inclusion of the right of resistance to oppression was controversial then and remained so forever afterward. Who may define oppression? Is it an objective or a subjective definition? Who may decide the degree to which resistance is legitimate? The revolutionaries of Paris have taken heart from this phrase for more than 200 years. The feminist revolutionary Olympe de Gouges, for example, wrote in 1791 that for women, resistance to oppression is, in fact, the most important right.

Some provisions of the French Declaration merely restate traditional notions of property rights. Article 3 states that all sovereignty resides in the entire body of the nation, meaning all the people. Article 4 defines liberty as "power to do whatever does not harm others." This is a classically liberal, negative statement of the limits of liberty.

Article 10 provides for the free exercise of religion. Article 11 provides for free speech and a free press. Article 12 is an innovation in protecting property rights: It provides that the public force (e.g., the police) must be used for public and not private purposes.

The introduction to principles of taxation in the Declaration is important: Article 13 states, "For the support of the public force, and for the expenses of administration, a communal contribution is indispensable; it must be equally shared among all citizens, taking account of their capacities."

The abuse of the taxing power was one of the principal causes of the public reaction against the Ancien Régime in France. This provision seems to assure that all citizens would share in an equal tax burden, possibly with blanket exemptions for the poor. That Robespierre later felt compelled to speak out against this provision because of its lack of progressivity suggests that a mandate for equality of taxation is the correct interpretation.

Article 14 elaborates on taxation. This provision nominally gives French citizens greater rights to inquire into the public accounts than usually is the case under Anglo-American law, by granting them the right to question the necessity of taxation and to determine the "rate, incidence, collection, and duration" of a tax. In contrast, in modern America, the courts consistently have ruled for at least 50 years that taxpayers have no standing to bring lawsuits against tax laws or other government policies. The same observations apply to Article 15 of the Declaration, which authorizes "society" to demand an accounting from public agents for their administration.

Restating arguments taken from Montesquieu, Article 16 strengthens property rights by declaring unconstitutional the failure to assure the guarantee of rights or to define and separate the powers of government.

Article 17 delivers the same (perhaps even a greater) degree of protection to private property as does the Fifth Amendment taking clause of the U.S. Constitution.

All the best of the Lockean classical liberal elements appear in it. Property is deemed sacred and inviolable by the state. No one shall be required to suffer its loss or loss of use. Eminent domain is limited to evident and legally proven public necessity (in contrast, considerations shading toward mere convenience might suffice in the United States today), and the state's exercise of eminent domain requires just compensation.

But the poor and the propertyless among those fighting for the French Revolution were not necessarily sacrificing their lives in order to win such sweeping protection for property. At least, the radical leaders who eventually seized control of the Revolution did not think so. It is no wonder that, in addition to speaking out àgainst equally apportioned taxation (Article 13), the radical Robespierre felt compelled to attack property as an institution in his famous speech of April 24, 1793.

ROBESPIERRE'S SPEECH

The early leaders of the French Revolution were enlightened aristocrats— Lafayette, Mirabeau, Condorcet, and other classical liberals who favored a constitutional monarchy under Louis XVI. The general view of the king was that he was somewhat ineffectual and easily misled by bad counselors. But on the whole, he was not considered a bad fellow and had the good fortune occasionally to select intelligent and politically astute counselors, such as the foreign minister Vergennes and the finance minister Necker. Queen Marie-Antoinette, however, had a train of advisers whom Jefferson particularly thought pernicious to the king's long-run interests and to the interests of the French nation.

As the French Revolution progressed, its more moderate leaders either were imprisoned (Lafayette) or died (Mirabeau, Condorcet, and Danton), not always by natural causes. The radical leader Maximilien Robespierre (1758-1794) became one of the rulers of France—and arranged for his rival Georges Danton to be guillotined April 5, 1794.

In early 1793 in the midst of the transition from a monarchy to a republic (the king was guillotined in January 1793), there were food riots in Paris over the prices of grain and bread. The National Convention, the ruling revolutionary government, debated proposals to make the rich provide a "forced loan" to the nation and to impose price controls on bread and other basic commodities. With this, the conception of property spelled out in the French declaration was turned on its head. Property no longer was a sacred right that could not be seized without just cause and fair compensation. Quite to the contrary.

When Robespierre took the podium April 24, he condemned the concept of property as the Convention had considered it thus far, which was more or less in line with traditional classical liberal ideals. Because of its long-lasting consequences, it is the most important anti-property rights speech in history. In it, Robespierre said, in part:

> I asked to speak . . . [to propose] to you first several articles that are necessary to complete your theory on property. Please do not let this word frighten anyone. *Ames*

de boue! [Souls of mud] who only value gold, I do not at all want to draw upon your hoards, however impure their source might be. You should know that this agrarian [reform, or land redistribution] law, of which you have spoken so much, is only a phantom created by troublemakers to frighten fools; surely we did not need a revolution to teach the universe that the extreme disproportion of fortunes is the source of many evils and much crime, but we are no less persuaded by that disproportion that equality of property is a dream. As for me, I believe that property is still less necessary for private happiness than it is for public happiness. The question is more one of rendering poverty honorable than to forbid opulence. . . .

Ask the merchant in human flesh what property is. He will tell you, while pointing out this long funeral box that he calls a ship, where he has fastened up and clapped irons onto men who appear to be alive: There is my property, he will say, I bought them for so much per head. Ask this other gentleman, who has lands and vassals, or who believes the universe turned upside down since he no longer has any, and he will give you more or less the same ideas of property. . . .

In the eyes of all men such as these, property is not dependent on moral principles. Why does your declaration of rights seem to present the same error?

Robespierre proposed to reform the traditional system of property rights by establishing four principles.

The first proposal is the most striking in its contrast to classical liberal ideals: Each citizen has a right to property, but that right is limited to the things guaranteed by law. In other words, in the absence of a state guarantee, there are no certain property rights.

The second proposal limits property rights by the obligation to respect the rights of others. In fundamental conceptions of classical liberal theory (that tend toward anarchy), a property owner should have an absolute right to use or dispose of the property as he or she sees fit. By the 1790s, especially in France, the use of property was limited to the extent that profitable or efficient alternatives to that use existed that avoided impairing someone else's quiet enjoyment of his or her own property.

The third proposal is similarly opposed to traditional property rights. It explicitly states that no one may prejudice the safety, liberty, existence, or property of others similarly situated. That is, colloquially stated, "My rights stop at the end of your nose." The qualifying concept of "similarly situated," however, seems to imply that if an individual's civil liberties were unequal, as would be the case for residents of foreign origin or conceivably for women, then a person having superior rights or the state itself could invade that individual's safety, life, liberty, or property as long as the requirements of due process were observed.

Robespierre's fourth principle of property rights reform declares that all ownership or trade that threatens the "safety, liberty, existence, or property of others" is invalid.

Robespierre further attacked traditional property rights by demanding a provision in the Declaration of Rights that would call for progressive taxation. "Now, for public contributions to common expense," he told the Convention, "is there a principle more self-evidently rooted in the nature of things and in eternal justice than the principle that imposes on citizens the obligation to contribute to public expenses progressively according to the extent of their fortunes, that is, according to the advantages that they derive from society?"

The contemporary French historian Lucien Jaume writes of this speech that Robespierre "...provided the master reference for the socialist movements of the following century. In his presentation, he spoke harshly of the Girondist [moderate socialist] movement and Condorcet's new [classical liberal] draft of a declaration...

"Defending natural law, but excluding property from it, Robespierre was condemning with a simultaneous curse the whole Girondist movement (which still was divided on this question)." Jaume continues. "The Incorruptible One wanted to create a symbol, and the ultimate fate of his legend shows that he succeeded in doing so."

As the 18th-century feminist writer Germaine de Stael (1766-1817) put it, the wrong turn in the Revolution wrought by Robespierre and his Jacobin or Montagnard followers (the "Men of the Mountain") in the Convention arose from a misapplication of the ideas of Jean-Jacques Rousseau (1712-1778) , the French philosopher whose *Social Contract* (1762) helped inspire the French Revolution. Rousseau had an *ideal* that inspired many subsequent writers: human equality and the surrender of one's individual identity in order to regain it by "voluntarily" agreeing to its subjection to the general will. Robespierre, in contrast, had an *agenda*, an action plan, drafted in 38 articles to replace the original classical liberal Declaration of Lafayette (1789) and the revised, still classically liberal, Declaration prepared by Condorcet (1791).

Robespierre was the first to stand before a fully empowered national legislature and demand the recasting of property rights as dependent on the will of the state, a moral test for property ownership (we might say today, a test for political correctness), and a sharp, slashing demand for progressive taxation.

The doctrines he espoused, including a revolutionary, redistributive doctrine of property rights and a demand that all taxation be progressive became widespread in Europe during and after the reign of Napoleon I (1799-1815, with interruptions). In their extreme form, Robespierre's (or Rousseau's) ideas became the basis of continental European socialist doctrines about property for the next 200 years. Decades later, for example, the French social theorist Pierre Proudhon (1809-1865) wrote, "Property is the right of exclusion and theft" and also a "despotic power."

Robespierre's influential ideas notwithstanding, the Revolution that he helped to lead into its most violent years eventually turned against him. Having sent thousands to the guillotine or the firing squad during the Reign of Terror, he himself was guillotined on July 28, 1794. Only he was executed facing upward, forced to watch the blade in its fatal descent.

BENTHAM AND THE RISE OF UTILITARIANISM

In England during these revolutionary years, the forefather of another dominant model of political economy, utilitarianism, was writing his first widely read book. Over the next century, this model would challenge and indeed largely displace classical liberalism as the governing principle of property rights in the United States and much of Western Europe. The author was Jeremy Bentham (1748-1832), and the book was *Introduction to the Principles of Morals and Legislation*, published in 1789.

Utilitarianism is an ethical theory that holds that the greatest good is the sum of happiness of the greatest number, or the greatest degree of happiness achievable for the greatest number. Happiness equals pleasure, the opposite of pain. According to Bentham's theory, pleasures should be measured by such factors as their intensity, duration, and probability of recurrence.

Utilitarianism may be called *positive* liberty—the freedom to achieve happiness or some other good—as distinguished from *negative* liberty, or freedom from being coerced or otherwise limited in thought or action by others. The latter is the essence of classical liberalism.

Leaders of the French Revolution liked Bentham's book so much that they made him an honorary French citizen (as they did Thomas Paine and George Washington). Bentham found this ironic because he was personally opposed to some (but by no means all!) of the works of the Revolution. Bentham's ideas have great intellectual influence to this day. Most mainstream American economists (especially neoclassicals), law professors, and judges are utilitarians of one stripe or another. This has important implications for property rights.

The theory of utilitarianism was further advanced by John Stuart Mill in his book *Utilitarianism* (1859). His principal refinement was to focus on the moral *quality* of the pleasures measured. One might value more highly the pleasure of philosophical contemplation than the pleasure of certain foods, for example, and deduce that the contemplative life is superior to the life of a *gourmand* (or even of a *gourmet*).

The intellectual appeal of utilitarianism lies in its supposedly logical and regular character, depending as it does on measurement. Yet a frequent criticism, and one that Mill himself acknowledged and attempted to address, is that *utility* measurement cannot necessarily answer *quality* questions. Such questions require decisions based on personal judgment and taste, which dyed-in-the-wool utilitarians tend to dismiss as "mere units of gratification," because they can make no objective distinctions among them.

Ultimately, a true utilitarian asks that an issue be *quantified* before he can understand it properly; a true classical liberal would ask that it be *qualified* (by historical derivation or moral comparison, for example) before any judgment is made. A utilitarian view of contested property rights might award them to the individual or society of persons offering the greatest objective value (the highest price) for them. A classical liberal view of those rights would begin its inquiry with an examination of the historical and legal basis for the assertion of each right.

Classical liberals acknowledge that *efficiency* is necessary *but not sufficient*. Utilitarians often are more inclined to cease their inquiry once the proper measurements of efficiency are established. It is in this sense that classical liberals claim to see the moral content in things, while utilitarians often find moral comparisons difficult to make (hence the pursuit of supposedly "values-neutral" economic research, for example).

For the purposes of this study, the important point is that utilitarians are far more willing to invade property rights in the name of the greater good than are classical liberals, who tend to be more absolutist about property rights. The main problem of modern Anglo-American jurisprudence and modern American economics in dealing with contested property rights is a failure to understand that property rights present the problem of a square peg in a round hole problem. Utilitarian analysis cannot resolve fully the classical liberal objections to compulsory transfers of property rights, and those objections tend to strike utilitarians as mere obstinacy that can be brushed aside in the pursuit of efficiency.

Bentham was influenced by somewhat contradictory streams of thought derived from Rousseau, the English law teacher and Tory philosopher William Blackstone (1723-1780), the Scottish philosopher David Hume (1711-1776), and the French philosopher Claude Helvétius (1715-1771). Helvétius has been described as one of the supreme "sensualists" in philosophy. (His widow later lived with Benjamin Franklin in Paris.) The 20th century French historian Elie Halévy credits Helvétius (but one also could credit Rousseau) with inspiring the following lines of Bentham:

> …the business of government is to promote the happiness of the society, by punishing and rewarding. . . . [The magistrate operates] in the character of a tutor upon all the members of the state, by the direction he gives to their hopes and to their fears.

Bentham tried to apply objective criteria to what Halévy calls "the art of morals and legislation." The evolution of that effort has led utilitarian inquiry into such fields as modern behavioral psychology and behavioral economics. Bentham studied law at Oxford with Blackstone, but he claimed not to have accepted Blackstone's historically based analysis of the common law. He wrote that he preferred to look at law as it should be, not as it was.

His teachings on property law begin nicely from the standpoint of classical liberal ideas. He wrote that the definition of the right of property is the chief object of civil law. He asks: "…what is justice but the respect for the right of property once that right has been defined?"

The main problem for utilitarians attempting to justify social intervention in property rights in the name of the greater good is that Locke, who could be deemed a property rights absolutist, also founded his theory of property on utility (the value of a man's labor). Bentham is hard-pressed to find anything other than labor on which to found his own utility theory of property.

Bentham also believed that the proper aims of the civil law of property should be the pursuit of security and equality. The principle of security is the foundation of property and counts for more than equality. Or as Halévy wrote of Bentham's work: "Property is the justified *expectation* of drawing certain advantages from the thing which you think you possess; it is not a physical reality but a belief set up as a certainty."

Property also is an *expectation* that the law should not destroy, once created. In the interest of preserving this expectation, what *distribution* should be pursued? Bentham's answer: The one that already exists.

To the extent that Bentham exalts security, he is a legal traditionalist and a conservative, reasonably congenial to Lockean classical liberals regarding property rights. But to the extent that he exalts gradual equalization in the name of the greater good, he more closely approximates the ideals of the moderates of the early phase of the French Revolution or, say, Thomas Jefferson among our own Founding Fathers. There is a tendency in modern utilitarianism to divide in a crisis toward "equalitarian communism" or "hereditary traditionalistic principles." But for Bentham there was no doubt: Equality must give way to security. Besides, he believed, true equality is a chimera. As Halévy wrote: "the only thing which can be done is to lessen inequality."

Through the influence of ideas similar to Bentham's espoused about the same time by Alexander Hamilton and, later, Henry Clay, Daniel Webster, Chief Justice John Marshall, and others, a strongly utilitarian view of property rights emerged in the American legal tradition. This view weighed the advantages and disadvantages of particular governmental interventions in property rights (or in creating new forms of property) and protected *business* (fictive or incorporeal) interests in property as distinct from the property interests of *individuals* (or in Colonial times, the Crown). In contrast, the classical liberal view of property rights, as derived from Locke, has been that property rights are fundamental and absolute and that government has no right to override them by not paying for any taking.

Both utilitarianism and socialism, the two major competing ideologies about property that emerged around the time of the French Revolution, are arrayed *against* Enlightenment-era classical liberalism of the Lockean variety.

Robespierre and the state-centered theory of property rights advocated moral tests for property rights, progressive taxation, and an aggressive pursuit of absolute equality of men's estates. Bentham and the utilitarians preferred security over equality, but they grounded security on non-traditional bases and constantly strove for greater equality. Locke would have resisted any redistribution of property at all, so long as "reasonably as good" was still left in the commons for the next fellow to exploit. Bentham would have opposed Robespierre on any final plan of aggressive redistribution of land or other property among the living.

All persons living today in the industrial economies, especially in the United States, and particularly persons subject to eminent domain takings or to adverse property use under zoning laws, are still dealing with the legacies of these two late 18th century sets of competing ideas, socialism and utilitarianism, regarding property rights.

ORIGINS OF CORPORATISM OR STATISM

The fourth and final model of property rights and political economy is corporatism, or statism. For many readers, the word "corporatism" will call to mind corporations. But as a political or economic model, corporatism (from the Latin word *corpus*, meaning body) refers to the organization of society into bodies—associations, unions, government agencies, businesses, and, yes, corporations—that exert some control over individuals. Statism is, for Americans, a more familiar term to express this sort of control. It is a neologism, a term that came into general use only following World War II. The term corporatism more broadly captures the intended role of non-state bodies. There are two varieties of corporatism (with considerable overlap): European and American.

European corporatist doctrines arose in the 19th century in reaction to both classical liberal and Robespierrean socialist ideas. The standard study attributes the origin of corporatism (or at least its variant *fascism*, which is corporatist economic ideas married to an aggressively nationalistic foreign policy, backed by the military means of executing that policy) to certain French legitimist (royalist or pro-Bourbon) exile writings after the French Revolution.

The main components of 19th-century corporatist doctrines included such things as the establishment of publicly financed social insurance for the general population. These and other policies were encouraged by political movements associated with the Catholic Church in Western Europe, and by the established Protestant churches of northern Europe, after the European Revolutions of 1848. Corporatism was seen as a morally acceptable alternative to the agnosticism and potential for class warfare believed inherent in the rising socialist ideas of the day. The principal objective of corporatism was to reduce or eliminate economic competition, introducing central economic planning to the extent necessary to achieve this goal, as a means of avoiding the class warfare believed inherent in classical, *laissez-faire* systems.

By 1871, in the large continental nations (Germany, Italy, and France), mildly or strongly corporatist ideas held sway. Community interests prevailed over individual preferences with respect to property. Government favored central economic planning. Society was organized along the lines of the medieval guilds (now called trade unions, trade associations of businesses, and agricultural cooperatives). National cooperation against external competitors took precedence over internal economic competition. The beginnings of the modern welfare state arose, featuring state-chartered, state-regulated, state-subsidized, and sometimes state-owned corporations.

In 20th century Europe, the main battleground of ideas was between European socialism, and the European or American varieties of corporatism or statism. But with both, the dominant idea was to compete abroad as one undifferentiated national economic unit. Great Britain adopted the ideals of the modern welfare state in the aftermath of World War II (the principal advocate was the economist William H. Beveridge, 1879-1963).

Since the 1920s, Britain usually vacillated between two models of political economy. Under Labour governments, it followed a weak form of nominal *socialism* that resembled Benthamite utilitarianism. The 1990s, for example, saw the rise of Prime Minister Tony Blair's "third way," which incorporated less Marx or Beveridge and more Bentham. Tory governments generally refused to dismantle Labour's postwar welfare state and instead pursued moderate or American-style corporatism. Only when Margaret Thatcher became prime minister in 1979 did significant strains of British political rhetoric begun to honor classical liberal views again.

CORPORATISM IN AMERICA

In America as early as 1791, a proto-utilitarian view of property rights spawned governmental protection and promotion of corporations. That year Alexander Hamilton proposed the establishment of the Bank of the United States, a sort of central bank for the U.S. government. In the early part of the 19th century, the Federalist judiciary that was the principal legacy of John Adams' tenure as president began to sustain the property rights claims of the new legal entities that the states were creating.

Steamboat monopolies on the Hudson River, toll bridge monopolies on the Charles River, eminent domain claims of canal and, later, railroad companies all passed through a constitutional filter in John Marshall's Supreme Court, which ran from 1801 until Marshall's death in 1835. The usual decisions of the Marshall court amounted to encouragement of new corporate charters (an efficiency-promoting and pro-competitive measure) and a general permissiveness regarding the types and amounts of property that corporations could own and control. States were limited in the countermeasures that they were allowed to take against out-of-state corporations because the Marshall court interpreted the commerce clause of the Constitution as pre-empting state action in the regulation of interstate commerce.

The expansive ways the courts interpreted corporate charters would have astonished most of the Founding Fathers and probably most of the constitutional Framers. Indeed, these new policies can be reconciled only with utmost difficulty with the classical liberal theories of property that most of the Founding Fathers and the Constitution's Framers shared.

The American Civil War created fertile ground for the growth of what retrospectively could be described fairly as corporatism or statism. The first use of a steam locomotive on a railway in America was on a three-mile railroad in Honesdale, Pennsylvania, in 1829. By the Civil War, and for several decades afterward, railroad companies were the most important American corporations. After the war, in order to create a transcontinental railroad network, Congress granted the railroads 20 square miles of land for every mile of track that was laid. For the first time in American history, corporations other than land companies controlled land that was not an integral part of their physical plants. The courts allowed this expansive use of corporate powers.

In the immediate aftermath of the Civil War, New York's Roscoe Conkling (1829-1888) served on a U.S. House of Representatives committee that drafted the 14th Amendment. Ratified in 1868, it granted all Americans the same privileges, immunities, and rights to equal protection and due process. These clauses ordinarily would be read as vindications of the political rights and civil liberties of the recently freed African-American slaves. But Conkling, a railroad bond lawyer who also controlled the Republican Party patronage machine in New York State, allegedly performed the first large-scale sleeper operation of American history. He (or his drafting committee) made the exact phraseology describing the entities covered by the 14th Amendment to vary between *persons* and *citizens*.

Years later, representing a railroad before the U.S. Supreme Court (*Santa Clara County v. Southern Pacific Railroad*), Conkling argued essentially that the draftsmen of the amendment (and he should know because he was one of them) intended the particular distinctions between *person* and *citizen*. He argued that the railroad was a *person* (albeit corporate and fictive) who was a corporate *citizen* of the United States and therefore was entitled to the equal protection of the laws. The Supreme Court so held in 1886. After a brief discussion on the bench, the Justices stated that they merely assumed that this outcome already was settled law. This historic ruling conferred upon corporations the same constitutional property rights that ordinarily pertained to natural persons.

In the 1880s, building on similar legal foundations, John D. Rockefeller and his partners in what became the Standard Oil Company organized the first holding companies, which were organized specifically to hold controlling shares of other corporations. When the federal government attacked these holding companies as monopolies under the Sherman Anti-Trust Act of 1890, Rockefeller's attorneys then devised the first voting trusts. These bound all the members of the trust to vote their corporate shares for common objectives or for a common slate of directors, thereby accomplishing the objectives of a holding company indirectly. By the 1890s, J.P. Morgan and Co. (a banking partnership that owned shares of corporations and participated in voting trusts) was an anti-trust problem of a magnitude comparable to Standard Oil. Congress enacted the Clayton Act amendments in 1914 to strengthen the Sherman Act against these and other trusts.

In protest of the "corporate protectionist" view of property that dominated American political economy after the Civil War, there arose divergent, non-classical lines of attack. In 1879, self-taught economist Henry George inspired a political movement with the publication of *Progress and Poverty*, which proposed a single tax—on undeveloped land and land treated as if undeveloped—to finance government. Two years later, journalist Henry Demarest Lloyd published an expose of the oil industry and Standard Oil in the Atlantic Monthly that marked the beginning of a 25-year career as a spokesman and sometime political candidate calling for reform and income redistribution. In 1904, following in Lloyd's muckraking tradition, journalist Ida M. Tarbell continued the attack on corporate expansionism with *The History of the Standard Oil Company,* which helped bring about the 1911 break-up of Standard Oil of New Jersey under the Sherman Antitrust Act. Also during this period, future Supreme Court Justice Louis D. Brandeis began articulating the origins of modern anti-trust theory.

The "protected" interests during this era denounced all these reformers as "socialists" (the Duke of Argyll called George a "communist," for example), but none of them (with the possible exception of Lloyd, with his strong redistributionist bent) would have warmed Lenin's heart.

Overall, the reforms of the Progressive Era (roughly 1892-1916) did very little to reduce the significance or influence of corporations as property owners in America. Instead, corporations were able to obtain certain protections of their property interests, such as high tariffs and subsidies, that ordinarily would not be available to individual citizens. All of this was a far stretch from the original constitutional conception of property rights in America.

The New Deal, wartime economic planning, and the Great Society programs of the 1960s did little to slow the rising corporatism of American public policy.

During the New Deal, the Federal Reconstruction Finance Corporation (RFC) made loans to and purchased the preferred stock of most significant American corporations. The RFC made $50 billion (or approximately $817 billion in today's dollars) of loans, guarantees, and preferred stock purchases over a 13-year period ending with the close of World War II. In many instances, the RFC selected the managements of the borrowing corporations as a condition of approving the loans. In other words, the executive branch of the Federal government appointed the managements and invested in a large portion of corporate America. This raises the question, who exactly owned or controlled the property of those corporations during that time?

Similar arrangements have been a feature of national defense procurement since 1950, and defense workers ordinarily are prohibited from striking under federal law, an example of private companies being subject to a level of government influence usually associated with state ownership.

Some might view the American New Deal of the 1930s as a triumph of Marxist influence on the federal government. But New Deal legislation and regulations were drafted mainly by non-Marxist lawyers and economists drawn from the largest banks, corporations, and private universities. As Henry Hazlitt, the libertarian economist and journalist, wrote more than a half century ago:

> ...government "aid" to business is sometimes as much to be feared as government hostility. This applies as much to government subsidies as to government loans. The government never lends or gives anything to business that it does not take away from business. One often hears New Dealers and other statists boast about the way government "bailed business out" with the Reconstruction Finance Corporation, the Home Owners Loan Corporation and other government agencies in 1932 and later. But the government can give no financial help to business that it does not first or finally take from business. The government's funds all come from taxes.

When the government makes loans or subsidies to business, what it does is to tax successful private business in order to support unsuccessful private business.

REGULATION OF WESTERN LAND USE

The seeds of another debate over property rights were sown during the New Deal—the current problem of western land ownership. The Constitution seemed to contemplate (Art. IV, sec. 3, cl. 2) that Congress would provide rules for the disposition of federal lands. The Northwest Ordinance of 1787 had already set forth such a mechanism: Indian lands were to remain in the hands of the Indians, and whatever lands the Indians later ceded to federal control were to be surveyed for sale and settlement by the territorial governors.

However, particular problems have arisen regarding modern federal land use regulations under the U.S.-Mexican Treaty of Guadalupe Hidalgo (1848), by which the United States acquired most of the territory of the modern Southwest and settled the status of Texas. This treaty explicitly confirmed the pre-eminence of prior private Spanish, Mexican, and Indian land titles and water rights. In addition, in 1872, Congress established Yellowstone as the first national park. For the first time, this gave the federal government permanent ownership of lands not used for armories, office buildings, forts, and military bases.

Pending sale of federal lands in the West (the only open lands remaining after the Indian Territory in Oklahoma was opened for settlement in 1889), the federal government leased property to ranchers, mining companies, and others willing to use it for economic activity. Gradually, federal lands were sold off, but such sales were halted under the economic emergency measures of the New Deal and never were resumed. Consequently, states such as Nevada and Utah still have very high proportions (84 and 57 percent, respectively) of their land in federal hands. And from the Rocky Mountain States westward the norm is that 35 percent or more of the land is owned by the federal government.

In the East, New York or Ohio, for example, federal ownership of 1 or 2 percent of a state's land is the norm. The impact of federal land ownership on state governance and tax bases in the West is far more serious than most Easterners understand. Purely as an economic proposition, continued federal control of Western lands is puzzling. If our study demonstrates anything, it is that efficient and sustainable land use requires that individual (or even corporate) property rights be assigned and that private actors, not governments, be the principal land holders.

THE EXPANSION OF MODERN AMERICAN CORPORATISM

A strong variety of corporatism, combined with the beginnings of a modern welfare state, reached its high water mark in the mid-1930s. The welfare state resumed expansive growth during Lyndon Johnson's Great Society years (1964-1968). Richard Nixon then expanded the welfare state further in the guise of the New Federalism (1969-1973).

Only after the election of Ronald Reagan as president in 1980 was public attention directed again toward classical liberal rhetoric. However, the Reagan administration gave only slipshod execution of classical liberal economic policies.

The closeness of the 2000 American election suggested that the American public remained divided on whether it wanted bigger or smaller, or more active or less active, government. There appeared to be no consensus on any number of public policy issues—including property rights—or if a consensus is emerging, it seems to be pro-corporatist.

Which theory of property rights does the public endorse, after all: state-centered, corporation-centered, community-centered, or individual-centered? The answer is simply not clear.

More recently, the economic turmoil that emerged in August 2007 and burst into public view with the failure of the Bear Stearns investment bank in March 2008 seems to have pushed policy and opinion farther into the pro-corporatist camp. In the name of bailing out important sectors of the economy, the federal government has committed hundreds of billions of taxpayers' dollars to helping out and acquiring ownership of private corporations.

Federal Reserve and Treasury obscurantism regarding the size, duration, and collateral for their funding efforts for failing enterprises has tended to shield the vast amounts involved from public view. But it is not unreasonable to value the amounts already spent (probably between $2 and $3 trillion) together with promises of future assistance outstanding at about $10 trillion. These are expenditures and promises that did not yet exist in early March 2008. For comparison, U.S. gross domestic product is about $14 trillion.

Nearly all the funds provided for crisis relief are aimed at propping up corporate balance sheets; very few are aimed at individuals. Corporations were able to obtain this relief on terms and conditions not otherwise available to individuals. Whether this signifies a temporary response to an emergency or a redefinition of the proper role of government regarding property rights remains to be seen.

What is clear however it that the evolution of property rights, particularly corporate property rights, in the modern era after 1800 has created a number of economic and constitutional problems. The ancient traditions of property rights—the source of the classical liberal view—arose from and were aimed at protecting the interests of individual property owners. But in the modern world, corporations have stronger property rights than individuals. Corporations even can marshal the eminent domain power of the state to take private property from individuals for corporate purposes, notwithstanding what the Constitution and ancient customs actually say on this point.

Similarly, government has the capacity to use land use zoning or eminent domain takings to deprive existing land holders of the beneficial use of their property. In modern times, the government increasingly has done this in response to pressures from prominent individuals or corporations. Agricultural policy has further contributed to the weakening of private property rights. Since 1933, land owners have traded control of the beneficial use of their property for governmental regulation of that use combined with governmental subsidies typically paid out in five-year installments. (There has been a succession of five-year plans for American agriculture since the early 1950s).

At the end of the day, however, corporations are creatures of the state. They did not exist originally at common law. As with all creatures of the state, what the state giveth, the state can take away. To prevent such deprivation of benefit, corporations have powerful incentives to attempt to control the state itself, for mere self-protection if not for any more malevolent purpose. Utilitarian analysis (a mere balancing of costs and benefits of governmental action affecting property rights) can be a sword cutting in more than one direction regarding land-use zoning, eminent domain, and corporate property rights generally. It is left to the reader to judge whether, when, and to what extent corporations have acted in response to incentives to influence or control the state in the post-New Deal United States.

For a while, at least before the post-2007 financial crisis, socialist theories of property (especially features like state or community ownership of the means of production) seemed unlikely to make much headway in the United States. However, corporatism or statism remains an ever-present temptation to governing elites, because of the facility for state- or corporate-directed central planning and social control that it offers. Thus, modern corporatism, even in the moderate form usually encountered in industrial economies (often under the euphemism, "mixed economy"), remains a peril to individual liberties and property rights. Meanwhile, utilitarian notions that have been transformed into modern welfare liberalism probably still are the dominant ideology of the day with respect to property rights in many, if not most, parts of the United States. They carry with them the potential to become as dangerous as full-blown corporatism for individual liberties and property rights.

The constitutionally supported view always was and still remains that of the classical liberal theory of property rights: Every free citizen has a natural right to acquire, possess, and enjoy property, to be protected in that enjoyment, and to dispose of his property according to his own free will. This is the only view explicitly supported in both the text of the U.S. Constitution and the history that led up to its adoption, as we have recounted in this study. Deviations from that ancient, Lockean, classically liberal view are, for the most part, modern innovations. They include efficiency-driven U.S. Supreme Court decisions and centrally planned, corporately influenced economic policies initiated since the New Deal. They have more to do with utilitarianism and corporatism than with respect for the classically liberal political economy models of the Founding Fathers and the Framers of the Constitution regarding property rights.

Subject Index

Name Index

About AIER

American Institute for Economic Research (AIER) conducts independent, scientific, economic research to educate individuals, thereby advancing their personal interests and those of the nation.

The Institute, founded in 1933, represents no fund, concentration of wealth, or other special interests. Advertising is not accepted in its publications. Financial support for the Institute is provided primarily by the small annual fees from several thousand sustaining members, by receipts from sales of its publications, by tax-deductible contributions, and by the earnings of its wholly owned investment advisory organization, American Investment Services, Inc. Experience suggests that information and advice on economic subjects are most useful when they come from a source that is independent of special interests, either commercial or political.

The provisions of the charter and bylaws ensure that neither the Institute itself nor members of its staff may derive profit from organizations or businesses that happen to benefit from the results of Institute research. Institute financial accounts are available for public inspection during normal working hours of the Institute.

The Benefits of
AIER MEMBERSHIP

If you enjoyed this book, you'll love AIER's newsletter publications. With a staff of expert researchers, AIER is able to offer valuable insight on a wide array of economic and personal finance issues.

Research Reports provide concise discussion concerning a wide range of current issues. One article each month is devoted to analyzing changes in economic activity.

Economic Bulletins present in-depth treatment and analysis of topics pertaining to economics, fiscal policy, retirement, and personal finance.

For more information about AIER membership, **please call us toll free at (888) 528-1216.**

Mention this publication to receive a discount on your annual membership fee. Sign-up online by visiting our website, www.aier.org

AIER

publications currently available

Personal Finance

The A-Z Vocabulary for Investors
Car Bargains: Best Used Auto Values
Coin Buyer's Guide
Homeowner or Tenant? How to Make a Wise Choice
How to Avoid Financial Fraud
How to Avoid Financial Tangles
How to Give Wisely: A Donor's Guide to Charitable Giving
How to Invest Wisely
How to Make Tax-Saving Gifts
How to Read a Financial Statement
How to Use Credit Wisely
If Something Should Happen:
  How to Organize Your Financial and Legal Affairs
Life Insurance: From the Buyer's Point of View
Sensible Budgeting with the Rubber Budget Account Book
Start Here: Getting Your FInancial Life on Track
What You Need to Know About Mutual Funds

Retirement And Estate Planning

The Estate Plan Book—with 2001 Supplement
How to Build Wealth with Tax-Sheltered Investments
How to Choose Retirement Housing
How to Cover the Gaps in Medicare:
  Health Insurance and Long-Term Care Options for the Retired
How to Plan for Your Retirement Years
How to Produce Savings in the Administration of an Estate
What You Need to Know about Social Security

Money And Banking

The Collapse of Deposit Insurance
Gold and Liberty
Money: Its Origins, Development, Debasement, and Prospects
The Pocket Money Book:
  A Monetary Chronology of the United States
Prospects for a Resumption of the Gold Standard

General Economics

The AIER Chart Book
The Constitutional Protection of Property Rights: America and Europe
Forecasting Business Trends
The Future of the Dollar
The Global Warming Debate: Science, Economics, and Policy
On the Gap between the Rich and the Poor
Progress and Property Rights: From the Magna Carta to the Constitution
Property Rights: The Essential Ingredient for Liberty and Progress
Prospects for Reforming the IMF and the World Bank
Reconstruction of Economics
The United States Constitution: From Limited Government to Leviathan